THE PROMISE AND THE PRICE

Women's studies books of related interest

Bureaucrats, Technocrats, Femocrats
Anna Yeatman

Dissenting Opinions
Regina Graycar

Educating Girls: *Practice and Research*
Edited by Gilah C.Leder and Shirley N.Sampson

Female Crime: *The Construction of Women in Criminology*
Ngaire Naffine

Feminine/Masculine and Representation
Edited by Terry Threadgold and Anne Cranny-Francis

For and Against Feminism: *A personal journey into feminist theory and history*
Ann Curthoys

Frogs and Snails and Feminist Tales: *Preschool children and gender*
Bronwyn Davies

Gender and Power: *Society, the Person and Sexual Politics*
R W Connell

The Gifthorse: *A Critical Look at Equal Employment Opportunity in Australia*
Gretchen Poiner and Sue Wills

Law and the Sexes: *Explorations in Feminist Jurisprudence*
Ngaire Naffine

Playing the State: *Australian feminist interventions*
Edited by Sophie Watson

Populate and Perish: *Australian Women's Fight for Birth Control*
Stefania Siedlecky and Diana Wyndham

Same Difference: *Feminism and Sexual Difference*
Carol Bacchi

Secretaries Talk: *Sexuality, Power and Work*
Rosemary Pringle

Sexual Subversions: *Three French feminists*
Elizabeth Grosz

THE PROMISE AND THE PRICE

The struggle for equal opportunity in women's employment

Clare Burton

ALLEN & UNWIN

Once again, to Racheal, Stephen and Kate

First published in 1991
Allen & Unwin Australia Pty Ltd
8 Napier Street, North Sydney, NSW 2059 Australia

National Library of Australia
Cataloguing-in-Publication entry:
Burton, Clare
  The promise and the price: essays on women and organisations.

  Bibliography.
  Includes index.
  ISBN 0 04 442286 5.

  1. Women — Employment — Australia.
  2. Affirmative action programs — Australia.   3. Women Executives —
  Australia. I. Title

331.40994

Library of Congress Catalog Card Number: 90—082309

Set in 10/11 pt Sabon by Setrite Typesetters, Hong Kong.
Printed by Chong Moh Offset Printing Pte Ltd, Singapore

Contents

Tables

Figure

Preface

The essays in this book were written over the period 1983–1989. Many of them began as conference papers and many of these were subsequently revised for publication in journals and books. All of them have been written as responses to and commentary on prevailing organisation practice and government initiatives in the field of women's employment.

Although there is reference in the essays, particularly in Part II, to equal employment opportunity programs as they affect people of non-English speaking background, Aboriginal people and people with a physical disability, the central focus of the essays is on women in employment and on gender as a structuring principle within work organisations.

Generally speaking, the essays have not been updated to take account of fresh developments in the field of practice or in the theoretical literature. The exception to this is the section on the statutory framework covering sex discrimination in employment (in chapter 11).

Chapter 1 began as two papers which were revised and brought together into a single piece, first published as 'Public and private concerns in academic institutions' in Politics Vol. 20 No. 1 (May) 1985.

One of the two original papers, 'Documenting the power structure in academic institutions' was presented at the Conference on Equal Employment Opportunity and Affirmative Action at Macquarie University in 1983 and was subsequently published in Equal Opportunities International (U.K.) Vol. 3 No. 1 (1984). The second paper, 'The politics of merit and the exercise of power: issues in the promotion of academic women to positions of influence' was presented at the Conference on Women in Educational Management: the Way Forward, at the University of New England in July 1984.

Subsequently, the revised paper was altered again away from the focus on academic institutions and was published in 1986 in N. Grieve and A. Burns (eds) Australian Women: Feminist Perspectives for the Eighties (Melbourne: Oxford University Press) as 'Equal Employment Opportunity Programs: issues in implementation'.

Chapter 2 also began at a conference at Macquarie University, the Defining Merit Conference held in September 1985. 'Merit and gender' was revised and presented in November that year at the Royal Australian Institute of Public Administration National Conference in Sydney. It was subsequently published as 'Merit and gender: organisations and the mobilisation of masculine bias' in the Australian Journal of Social Issues Vol. 22 No. 2 (May) 1987 and more recently in the book of the RAIPA Conference proceedings, Politicization and the Career Service edited by G. Curnow and B. Page, published by the Canberra College of Advanced Education and the NSW Division of RAIPA (Canberra, 1989).

Chapter 3 began as a paper delivered to the International Symposium on Australian Public Sector Management and Organisation held in Brisbane in July 1988 and was revised for publication in the book of the proceedings of the conference, Dynamics in Australian Public Management edited by A. Kouzmin and N. Scott (Melbourne: Macmillan, 1990).

Chapter 4 has not been published before. A version of it was presented at the Australian National University Centre for Continuing Education Seventh New Developments in Public Sector Management Conference on 'Public participation, pressure groups and public servants' in August 1985 as 'Diversity as a strategy for participation'. It has been revised for publication here.

Chapter 5 was prompted by the abolition of the Public Service Board in Canberra and appeared in the Canberra Bulletin of Public Administration, No. 52 (October, 1987) as 'Equal Employment Opportunity — a future? The consequences of government policy for EEO in the public service'. I have made some alterations to this paper, in particular to the list of indicators of effective EEO practice in agencies, a set of indicators which could be said to be, as well, a set of pre-conditions for the 'mainstreaming' of the EEO function.

Chapter 6 began with my involvement as a consultant with the Australian Public Service when it began an office restructuring process in 1987 under the terms of an efficiency and productivity agreement between the unions and the government in line with the wage-fixing principles prevailing at the time. At the end of 1987 I presented a two-day seminar to officers involved in the implementation of the office restructuring and went on to write up my views on the EEO implications of such restructuring, with particular emphasis on the job redesign process. The chapter began, then, as a paper, delivered many times to many audiences, the first occasion being at a seminar organised by the regional office of the Department of Industrial Relations for senior staff of Australian public service agencies in Brisbane in February, 1988.

Chapter 7 was written for the Conference, Public Sector Personnel Policies: Next Steps, sponsored by the Public Sector Management Institute, Monash University, in conjunction with the Public Service Board of Victoria (Melbourne, February, 1989). The proceedings of this conference have since been published in Public Sector Personnel Policies for the 1990's edited by D. Corbett, C. Selby Smith and R. Smith (Melbourne: Public Sector Management Institute, Monash University, 1989).

Chapter 8 was work commissioned by the Federal Affirmative Action Agency and was published as the third in their series of Occasional Monographs as Gender Bias in Job Evaluation (Canberra: AGPS Press, 1989).

Chapter 9 has not been published before and is based on several different papers I have presented at seminars and conferences — for example the Conference, Women and Work, Victorian Department of Labour, Melbourne, March 1988 — dealing with the value attached to women's work. In these forums I have discussed the process of implementing job evaluation systems and how to build into that process mechanisms for reducing gender bias.

Chapter 10 has not been published before, although I have drawn on the research material presented here for papers presented at seminars on performance appraisal (or assessment, at it is increasingly being called), in particular for NSW public sector personnel since taking up my position as Director for Equal Opportunity in Public Employment in the NSW Government.

Chapter 11 has an interesting history. It forms part of a report commissioned by the New Zealand Law Commission as part of their preparations for a New Zealand Government Report Towards Employment Equity: Report of the Working Group on Equal Employment Opportunities and Equal Pay in 1988. Jane Innes worked with me on the report and is the author of the Statutory Framework section. The section dealing with the 1972 Equal Pay Decision was subsequently incorporated into the National Pay Equity Coalition Submission to the 1988 National Wage Case (June 1988) and has thus had some public airing. The report to the New Zealand Law Commission is not reproduced here in full, as certain sections of it cover material and issues dealt with elsewhere in this book.

Acknowledgements

It would be impossible to detail all the contributions that people have made to the ideas presented in these essays. But particular people did comment on the various papers as they were developing. Alex Kouzmin and Nick Scott made comments and editorial changes to Chapter 3; Julian Foley in particular contributed ideas to Chapter 5; Sylvia Winters worked closely with me on the development of Chapter 6; Jane Bridge, Rosemary Hunter, Carmel Niland, Robert Parker and Howard Whitton commented on Chapter 7; Caroline Falls and other staff from the Affirmative Action Agency provided comment on Chapter 8; and, as previously mentioned, Jane Innes wrote the Statutory Framework section of Chapter 11.

As well, the statistical data in the last section of Chapter 11 was collected by Mary McLeod for the National Pay Equity Coalition Submission and incorporated into my report for the New Zealand Law Commission. Meredith Burgmann provided comment on this section.

Felicity Rafferty was very generous with her time, documentation and comments on the 1972 Equal Pay Decision section and Philippa Hall and Christine Short also provided useful comment.

The School of Financial and Administrative Studies at the then Kuring-gai College of Advanced Education provided funding for the research into a performance appraisal system detailed in Chapter 10.

Venetia Nelson, who has edited my published work in the past, did far more than edit this book. She worked through the material and revised, amended, deleted and linked various parts of the manuscript so that it could emerge as a coherent whole, divided into meaningful sections. Her editorial comments forced me to abandon a couple of papers and to 'make sense' of the rest. I am very grateful for the care and effort that Venetia has devoted to this work.

Introduction

This book documents some of the reasons why EEO programs for women have not delivered their expected outcomes. It explores an underlying source of inequality in the labour market: women are not accorded the same value as men in our society and the devaluation of women is carried through into the assessments of the work they perform. This underlying problem — the structural subordination of women — continues to generate inequalities in employment which cannot be addressed simply through programs concentrating on broadening women's employment opportunities.

One of the problems we have in sorting out what is required of EEO programs is that most people do not know about the range of issues that is actually involved. Those trained and practising in the field of management may or may not be familiar with the economic and sociological literature on the operation of the internal labour markets, with the broad range of feminist scholarship which cuts across traditional disciplinary boundaries, and with much of the sociological literature dealing with gender and work organisations. Few management schools in our universities and colleges take on this literature and develop students' understanding of the issues it raises. How then can we expect managers, when EEO programs are initiated, to understand most of what we are talking about? How can a middle manager be expected to be sensitive to the experiences of women at the workplace? How can we persuade people that their practices at work help to *constitute* gender relationships? that men and women don't come to the workplace with their gender identities sewn up, as it were? that what we do and how we do it at work re-creates, reproduces, reorganises, reconstitutes our masculine and feminine identities?

Without some radical restructuring of our perceptions, let alone our practices, the subordination of women will continue. Their life circumstances and their interests are subsumed under more dominant, more powerful interests, of an economic, administrative and political kind, and all are touched, nowadays, with the 'metamyth' of the rational organisation of resources. Apparent achievements are readily undermined. This undermining might be in another place, at another time, or perhaps in relation to another group of female workers. But no achievement is guaranteed to be extended. While women's place is culturally defined as centrally within the family rather than in the world of paid work, or while women are accepted at the workplace but only in places deemed appropriate for them, and these places are not where the power lies, progress has a fragile base.

The Federal *Affirmative Action (Equal Employment Opportunity for Women) Act* 1986, covering private sector companies with more than 100 employees and higher education institutions, State EEO legislation covering public sector organisations, introduced into New South Wales in 1980 and in South Australia, Victoria and Western Australia in 1984, and the *Public Service Reform Act* 1984 covering the Australian Public Service, require employers actively to promote the employment opportunities of women.[1] This is to be achieved through the removal of discriminatory practices and the development of programs and strategies to redistribute women across occupational groups and organisational hierarchies. The result is expected to be equal employment outcomes for women.

If we had to define or describe such outcomes for women, what would we say? Would we describe a labour market where women were evenly distributed across occupational and industry classifications and hierarchies, or would we emphasise fair employment practices, regardless of whether the result is a more even distribution of women in the labour market? Would we focus on the areas of women's traditional work, and reassess its value?

The answers to these questions are different, depending on one's view of the sources of inequality between women and men in society.

In one view, affirmative action is a temporary redress measure, through which women are compensated for past discriminatory practices and are helped to take their place in the world on a more equal footing. Affirmative strategies apply in educational and employment contexts, carrying with them no implications for other social arrangements, such as the family.

In another view, equity strategies in education and employment can only scratch the surface, as the requirement for them will be generated continuously by the inequalities embedded in various institutional arrangements and practices. This view leads to two different positions on the effects of EEO programs on women's subordinate status.

The first, expressed by Game (1984), questions whether the programs can be anything more than a 'liberal update' providing new and more subtle forms of patriarchal domination, while the second, provided by Eisenstein (1985), argues that EEO programs might be a critical leverage point for more fundamental social change.

Some of the issues — if addressed, Game argues that they would be genuinely subversive of the patriarchal order — revolve around the politics of skill and the value of, and relationship between, women's paid and unpaid work.

The related issue of pay equity, which concerns the value of women's *paid* work relative to men's, is not one that receives attention under EEO programs. It has had some recent exposure in the Australian industrial context, but, since the rejection in 1986 by the Australian Conciliation and Arbitration Commission of the concept of comparable worth, is struggling to have a place on the industrial relations agenda (see Chapter 11; see also Short, 1986; O'Donnell and Hall, 1988).

EEO programs, on the surface, offer a great deal to women. In conjunction with other initiatives addressing women's access to employment — among other things, the provision of work-related childcare, the wider availability of permanent part-time work, the ratification of ILO Convention 156 which requires 'each member [to] make it an aim of national policy to enable workers with family responsibilities to exercise their right to work, without discrimination . . .', and the gradual introduction of programs to facilitate women's re-entry into the labour market — the EEO policies of the Federal and State governments in Australia promise to deliver improved prospects for women in paid employment.

The recognition of skills shortages and the shrinking of the pool of young, skilled labour, too, are creating a changed environment within which women's participation in the labour market is discussed. Increasingly it is the case that the innovative programs which EEO policy has encouraged to develop are taking shape in the public and private sectors, not from a philosophic commitment to anti-discrimination measures in themselves, but from a realisation that more women, older workers and people from racial and ethnic minorities will have to be employed to meet recruitment needs during the 1990s.

But there are risks in relying on the economic incentive alone. Of course discrimination is an inefficient work practice. Of course people's skills and capacities are under-used while employers select from traditional and narrow recruitment pools. But this focus — on the human resources needs of enterprises — allows much that needs to be changed to be left intact, in particular, the 'masculine' values which predominate in work organisations in the public and private sectors, and to which women are expected to conform. Response to the economic imperatives is not necessarily translated into the broad EEO policy framework which needs to inform employment strategies and practices.

The view taken in this book is in sympathy with Game's analysis yet shares Eisenstein's view of the potential of EEO programs to open up more difficult issues and contribute to the shaping of a more egalitarian social order. It focuses, therefore, on some of the reasons that such programs are having limited effectiveness in delivering equitable employment practices and outcomes.

PART I
Gender and Power in Organisations: an Evaluation

1 Masculinity and femininity in the organisation

In order to document the real power in an organisation, we need, as Goffman argues, to consider

> whose opinion is voiced most frequently and forcibly, who makes the minor ongoing decisions apparently required for the co-ordination of any joint activity, and whose passing concerns are given the most weight. And however trivial some of these little gains and losses may appear to be, by summing them all up across all the situations in which they occur, one can see their total effect is enormous. The expression of subordination and domination through this swarm of situational means is more than a mere tracing or symbol or ritualistic affirmation of the hierarchy. These expressions considerably constitute the hierarchy; they are the shadow *and* the substance. (Goffman, 1979:6)

Because men have been playing internal organisational politics through both formal and informal structures since the very foundation of these structures, most organisations are saturated with masculine values. These values, derived from men's experience, massively contribute to women's inequality at the workplace. Whether because certain constructions of masculinity are built into the very definition of many jobs, or because certain positions, or qualifications for advancement, demand time and activity which assume the existence of domestic support, the present arrangements in work organisations represent the cumulative outcome of a series of bargains and compromises between various parties among whom women have not played a significant or influential part. The result might well be that

> the leaders who move to the top of an organisation are not necessarily the most capable or imaginative. Too often the mantle falls to the survivors of organisational politics: those who reflect the characteristics of the corporate mind, a mind trained to calculate but not feel, to value means over ends, and, above all, to

preserve power even at the expense of policy initiative. (Zaleznick and Kets de Vriès, 1975:4−5)

We are dealing with deeply held beliefs, perceptions and realities about masculinity and femininity, and with strongly held ideas about women's place and women's capacities. Despite good intentions to the contrary, and despite the fact that women's participation in the workforce has been increasing steadily, they continue to be perceived, as Edna Ryan puts it, as 'invaders in the work place', (Game and Pringle, 1983:7) a place which many men regard comfortably as their home.

Some far from recent contributions to the sociology of work remain valuable sources for understanding many of our concerns. For example, Theodore Caplow in 1954 made two assertions about basic cultural themes in our society: first, that it is disgraceful for a man to be directly subordinate to a woman, except in family or sexual relations; and second, that intimate groups, except those based on family or sexual ties, should be composed of members of one or other sex but not both—the principle of 'homosociability'. Such cultural values are not necessarily crystallised in coherent or explicit statements by individuals making choices and decisions. This makes it difficult to demonstrate their existence, let alone explain their sources, a point Caplow acknowledges. He suggests that 'we are forced to adopt a technique of the social anthropologists, which is to assert the universality of a cultural theme on the basis of personal observation, introspection, and what might be called circumstantial evidence in the literature' (Caplow, 1954:238).

We have, too, records of past practices which continue to have their effects on people's work behaviour and attitudes. For example, the Report of the Royal Commission on Public Service Administration, 1920, indicated that an important function of subordinated female employment was 'to release promising youths from duties which are largely routine, thus widening their scope for training and improving their prospects for advancement' (Deacon, 1983:178)

If masculinity is felt to be devalued by subordination to women, this will affect the distribution of opportunities through a host of small events in the way that Goffman describes. Some managers, asked their reaction to the idea of men working under a woman boss, have said, 'I would resent it', 'I would resign', 'It would be an indictment of the men employed', and 'I don't like the sort of woman who would want that sort of job' (Hunt, 1975). More telling, perhaps, from a survey conducted in America, was this comment: 'As for an efficient woman manager, this is cultural blasphemy' (Bowman et al., 1965:169). Not everyone will confess to these views, and not everybody holds them. But if they are in some respects dominant views, they create barriers to change because they are the very basis for active resistance.

Homosociability is an important outcome of notions about organisational life that are taken for granted, and it is one which Equal Employment Opportunity (EEO) plans are trying to address. The argument about homosociability has been presented by different writers on organisations for quite a long time, and is given recent expression by Lipman-Blumen (1976: 16) in connection with women and work. She defines 'homosocial' as 'the seeking, enjoyment and/or preference for the company of the same sex'. But Lipman-Blumen is not merely saying that people prefer, or feel more comfortable with, similar people. She explains the attraction of men to men in terms of the greater power and resources they have, relative to what women have to offer.

Everett Hughes argued in 1944 that an individual may possess all legitimate official criteria for appointment to a particular position, but be excluded from consideration because of a lack of other characteristics associated with traditional incumbents. He commented, 'what is operating ... is a second set of characteristics that facilitate the establishment of a broad-based relationship', one of mutual recognition and trust. Rosabeth Kanter in *Men and Women of the Corporation* (1977) quotes Wilbert Moore, writing in 1962 on the tendency of managers to guard power and privilege for those who fit in, for those they see as 'their kind'. He referred, perhaps unfortunately, to this as 'homosexual reproduction' within corporations, a process by which males reproduce themselves in their own image. Kanter, following Lipman-Blumen, prefers the phrase 'homosocial reproduction', meaning the selection of incumbents on the basis of social similarity. She relates this to the uncertainty in the administrative process and to the need to trust new recruits, to ensure a certain degree of predictability in their responses, to allow for planning in a coherent way without new perspectives being placed on problems which might lead to novel solutions upsetting the status quo. 'Trust' here encompasses mutual understanding based on the sharing of common values. To ensure it is to keep control in the hands of socially homogeneous peers, to prefer social certainty to the strains of dealing with people who are different. Kanter's research showed that women were placed quite clearly in the category of the incomprehensible and unpredictable. The whole question of females fitting into an organisation in positions of power and influence is overlaid with uncertainty. Men commented that communicating with them took more time, that they were hard to understand, and that with 'women's lib' around they never knew what to call them or how to treat them.

The fear of EEO lies deeper than just fearing more competition for jobs and promotional opportunities. Those who resist EEO fear something more than that: the very aspects of the work from which they derive most satisfaction are the aspects that could change considerably under an effective EEO program. My observations suggest that much satisfaction comes from wheeling and dealing, from feeling powerful and important, from the accumulation of the experiences of exerting influence. Further, part of the satisfaction in some jobs derives from the belief that it is *masculine* work, that women could not perform it adequately. I have heard of a man who said that if women were entering the carpentry trade, he would not like his son to take an apprenticeship, because it would be a sissy occupation. Another man, when asked how he would feel if women entered his own trade, said: 'some of the shine would go out of the job for me ... if I said to my mates I was working with a woman, they would feel, say, oh, he's doing a woman's job — because they can see that a woman *can* do it. They wouldn't think to say that she is the one who is doing a man's job.' (Cockburn, 1983:180)

This is the phenomenon the American literature refers to as 'tipping': as women enter an occupation, men leave. As Strober and Arnold (1987:11) point out, it is as important to ask why men leave as it is to ask why women enter, and they suggest that occupational segregation is less a matter of women's preferences and choices as it is a reflection of the power and status relationships between men and women.

One possible and economically rational reason can be given for men leaving as women enter an occupation. Many studies show that 'holding constant educational level, experience, job location and non-pecuniary job characteristics, the higher the percentage of women in an occupation, the lower the wage rate for both men and women in that occupation' (Strober and Arnold, 1987:117). This finding carries with it disturbing implications for EEO strategists. Generally speaking, it is believed that as more women enter male domains in organisations their position is more secure. Rosabeth Kanter (1977; 1980) is a well-known and influential advocate of the view that 'numbers have importance in and of themselves', that 'the problem of acceptance and effectiveness that many women encounter in managerial and professional occupations [may] derive primarily from their token status — the fact that there are, as yet, so few women in those positions' (1980:319). But it appears that, despite the level of acceptance that might be reached, the cost is lower pay and the lower status and influence associated with lower pay.

Graham Cleverley, in his *Managers and Magic* (1971), calls this strong feeling the fear of contagious effeminacy: men find less satisfaction in work once they discover women can do it. He finds it in men in the boardroom, in managers and administrators generally.

And I have heard other men comment that not only did they believe that as women entered their profession its status would be lowered but they also felt that if that were to happen they would value some of their work less, as they discovered that, after all, their capacity to perform it was not a reflection of their own masculinity. Some of the pride they took in their work would disappear if women could do the job.

This fear of too close an association with women was expressed recently in another context, by John Stone in a letter to the head of the New South Wales Ethnic Communities' Council, when he said:

> I refer to your letter . . . written in your (self-described) capacity as chairperson of the Ethnic Communities' Council of NSW. I should tell you frankly, at the outset, that any man so lacking in manliness as to describe himself as a chairperson is unlikely to command much respect from me. (*Sydney Morning Herald* 1 March 1988)

I call such strategies of resistance masculinity-protection strategies. Without the masculine connotation, the job ceases to be attractive to many men. Job satisfaction is then tied up with masculine ego satisfaction.

I am afraid we have to add to this dismal picture. For some men, the issue of long hours and weekend work is not viewed in the same light as it is viewed by the women who are tied to domestic responsibilities. The witching hour, for some men, is a time to be avoided. It is much more pleasant to go home after the kids have been bathed and fed. I am suggesting that some EEO initiatives will be resisted by men who wish to protect a position in the family which relies on the very sexual division of labour we are trying to break down: another component of masculinity-protection strategies, designed to protect a position at home as well as at work. Some of the apparent attractions of work reform along EEO lines — flexi-hours, parental leave, the very changes that take family life into account — may be unattractive to the present incumbents of the positions EEO strategies are trying to alter. For instance, the provision of childcare facilities can hardly be viewed as a positive benefit by men whose work expectations are already based securely on the knowledge that they are free of responsibility for childcare. Many men's lives are constructed in the context of material circumstances which, if fundamentally altered, would replace existing psychic rewards with little or nothing they value.

Elshtain argues that

> Because women have, throughout much of Western history, been a silenced population in the arena of public speech, their views . . . have either been taken for granted or assigned a lesser order of significance and honor compared to the public, political activities of males . . . politics is in part *an elaborate defense* against the tug

of the private, against the lure of the familial, against evocations of female power. (1981:15−16 emphasis added)

We are dealing with motivational and perceptual processes, both conscious and unconscious, some of which relate to cultural patterns emphasising the close association of women with parenthood and domestic concerns. The workplace as constructed by males is perceived as separate from this domain, both separate and entailing harder and more important work. They not only resist sharing in undervalued and unpaid work at the expense of the productive toil that goes to build their own careers, but they cannot afford to believe that women, doing both, can perform as well or better at the workplace. What would that say about their own progress, backed as it has been by domestic support? This problem is clearly exacerbated when women — the nurturers of small children — hold positions of authority over men at the workplace. Cultural blasphemy indeed, when our cultural and social traditions have emphasised not only the connection of women with dependence and subservience but the necessity for them to take the private, domestic load so that men could be free to engage in more important, public, affairs.

I am attempting, here, to integrate a set of related ideas, including Cleverley's suggestion that some organisational activity can be explained by men's fear of 'contagious effeminacy'. We need to understand why, when women present their views, they are regarded not only as of lesser significance, as Elshtain suggests, but as expressions of special interests, not even interests shared by all women, let alone by people more generally. Furthermore, women appear to be clamouring, quite incompetently, for changes in practices which, from the point of view of many men, are impossible, inconceivable and impractical. Such demands for change are taken in themselves to be the clearest possible evidence for the belief that women are indeed invaders at the workplace. They seem unable to comprehend what workplaces are all about, particularly when they seek to introduce arrangements more properly confined to the domestic sphere.

The reorganisation of 'public' activities to accommodate 'private' concerns could introduce new values to the workplace and lead to the expectation that men do things at work as well as at home that they have hitherto avoided as a waste of their time — activities using attributes such as conciliation and mediating skills, patience, supportiveness of people junior in rank, the sharing of responsibilities and information, the training of women in administrative and supervisory work, and other time-consuming activities offering few of the traditionally defined rewards. If Elshtain and Cleverley are correct, these changes might be viewed as potentially damaging to the scaffolding on which their masculinity is based.

My experience of a variety of types of organisations leads me to identify two contrasting approaches to the administrative process, broadly conceived. Negotiation is a central feature in the operation of organisations, where there are invariably some conflicts of interest and where considerable attention must be paid to the task of allocating scarce resources. One way of playing the negotiating game is for those with an established power base to block opportunities for others, and to use their power, based on past exchanges and inter-dependencies, to accumulate more power at the expense of other players. A central tactic is to exercise as much control as possible over the flow of information. The other way of playing the game, and I have seen it operate to the benefit of disadvantaged groups, is for those with power and experience of negotiating processes to encourage the participation of those groups who have been excluded in the past: to find out what they want, what their experiences have been and to bring them into the process of establishing the very frameworks for negotiating and compromise: in other words, to empower them.

What conditions allow for the latter situation? There are several, I believe. The first condition would be that democratic views prevail, that a hierarchy of power and privilege would not exist to mask the fact that some interests are given greater weight than others. The second follows from this: 'getting the numbers' would be based on people's equal capacity to exchange resources, to influence each other, to bargain and to negotiate. A third condition would appear to be that influential members feel that their competence derives from their ability to encourage the free expression of ideas and their capacity to allow for open negotiation between conflicting interests without 'losing' becoming a personal attribute. Not many work organisations fulfil these criteria.

A recent experience which increasing numbers of women are sharing relates to the emergence of women's networks or groups within occupations and organisations. Apart from those who might be familiar with collectives and collective modes of decision-making in the women's movement, more women are discovering the value of sharing experiences, particularly across occupational divisions (where we realise that apparently different circumstances share important, similar characteristics) and learning the value of compromise and negotiation so that a minimum negative impact is felt by any one category of people. This recalls an interesting piece of research carried out in the 1960s contrasting women's and men's strategy develop-ment in mixed-sex groups. In the games set up, 'males were found to play competitively, with strong motivation to win ... they strove to arrive at an outcome that will enhance their interests ... whereas females were more concerned with social and ethical considerations, oriented towards arriving at an outcome in the game maximally satisfactory (or fair) to all [...] participants' (Bond and Vinacke, 1961:61, 72). We have heard comparisons of this kind before; it is the interpretation that concerns me, as well as the practical issue of how we are going to tackle the consequences of the differences (see Kanter, 1980). How are we to affect the conditions of access to the opportunities to exert influence? Existing differences clearly reflect a social structure which has determined how much power men and women have had. The different socialisation processes are believed to equip women inadequately, relative to men, for the rigours of corporate life. More important than the *difference* in socialisation between girls and boys is the *experience* of the difference. The exclusion from activities and behaviours that are later rewarded within the workplace, the relative powerlessness *experienced* by girls and women, equip them in ways yet to be acknowledged at the workplace. Women are not biologically predisposed to be more sensitive than men to the needs of others. This is not a statement about women as women, but a statement about any category of people who have experienced subordinate status and the frustration of getting their concerns on any public agenda. They learn, through that, not individually as much as through collective action, the vital role that discussion, support, consultation and genuine hearings play.

The preceding comments partly answer a question which clearly needs to be addressed, which is why suitably qualified senior women have not been as forthcoming as we might expect in taking up opportunities to preside over important committees and to seek promotion to higher administrative and other positions. Whenever I am told that women are not putting themselves forward for promotion, and this is usually said as if this fact demonstrates their lack of willingness to take on extra responsibilities, or career commitments, or that it is something to do with womanhood, I ask, what are the conditions prevailing in the organisation to make this so? Many women are reluctant to take on positions which are so tightly ordered in hierarchical relationships that it would be a job in itself to change the system and the processes in order to make the administrative task as satisfying as some believe it could be, particularly by diluting the effects of hierarchy and generating more democratic processes. But it also has to do with the belief of many women that the style of administrative practice is of the first type described above. That is, they believe it to be a bit on the ugly side and they do not want to be part of an environment where decision-making seems more to do with point-scoring and the protection of existing status differences than with reasonable policy-making and implementation. Many women, through their experiences, show a preference and a capacity for supportive, mediating and negotiating styles sadly lacking in many men who hold positions of authority.

In the literature on women and work too much stress is put on women's general socialisation into dependency as a source of their subordination and too little emphasis is placed on the workplace itself. This dependency, I believe, is a component of the construction of masculinity and is represented within organisations by the typical relationship between boss and secretary. Women's unequal position at the workplace has been sustained partly by the legitimation of male authority through the rewards given for deference. Conventional gender assumptions inform the way relationships have been formalised and obscure the possibilities for change. As with many ideas, we have to turn on its head the idea that women are more suited to jobs requiring deference and view it from another angle. The construction of masculinity is such that many men seek deferential behaviour in others and have the power to bring it about, a behaviour buttressed by the notion of the importance of men at work as breadwinners, a powerful force sustaining a construction of femininity which gets in the way of women's strategic planning of their participation in the labour force.

This leads us to consider women's involvement in these processes. I find the notion of 'praxis traps' useful here, 'where people do things for good reasons and skilfully, in situations that turn out to make their original purpose impossible to achieve' (Connell, 1983:156). Cultural values affect in powerful ways the shaping of people's occupational planning and subsequent work lives. We have to ask, then, whether the lack of women in positions of authority is partly related to women's accommodative strategies in the labour market. That is, if notions of femininity, womanhood and good motherhood are not to be disturbed, women will organise their occupational choices and then, once on the job, their preferences for certain kinds of experiences, around those activities which do not challenge these dominant views. At the same time, if they are career-oriented, they may not have understood that these strategies have taken them in directions which do not lead to the sorts of opportunities they expected. This directs our attention to the definition and construction of the jobs themselves: if positions of authority are defined in instrumental, rational, impersonal or in highly political terms, rather than in supportive, facilitative, interpersonal and collaborative terms, women are less likely to aspire towards them. These ways of defining the work of people in authority are good ways of excluding women from it. While men on the whole perform this work, the issue of whether these are the most appropriate descriptions of what positions of authority entail remains clouded. Behind the scenes, among men, there is a great deal of support, facilitation and collaboration, processes not openly acknowledged as essential ingredients for adequate performance in leadership positions. The 'public' presentation of this work is all that women have access to; the 'private' understandings of the nature of the work are not readily available to them.

This is a double bind not only for women, in relation to the constraints of their feminine self-image. Males face the same dilemma in relation to their masculinity. When men aspire to positions of authority, they have had to place value on the repression of emotion; they have learnt to develop an impersonal approach to the job. To be subjected to female authority appears to make this process a waste of time. As Loring and Wells (1972:97) put it, 'if he accepts the prescribed unemotional manager's role, he can't accept women as managers', and neither is he going to welcome a change in the definition of the job which would erode his investment and his sense of the appropriateness of his masculine qualities to perform it.

So self-discrimination as a process requires elaboration, particularly in order to have incorporated within it the masculinity-protection source. Only if this happens will effective actions be capable of development to overcome the cause of the problem. Actions directed at women to compensate their weaknesses or inadequacies miss the point and leave current definitions of the administrative process and other types of work intact. The focus needs to be on institutional arrangements and organisational decision-making processes which perpetuate the male breadwinner complex of circumstances and which perpetuate views about appropriate job-holders, career paths, and organisational rewards. We need to think about organisational and occupational structures and the ways they have shaped the opportunities for women.

2 Organisations and the mobilisation of masculine bias

Chapter 1 has shown that the lower status of women in organisations is the result of motivational and perceptual processes within organisations that are in turn the product of basic assumptions about the nature and role of men and women. This chapter will explore the concepts of merit and skill as concepts basic to these assumptions.

The contribution of organisational processes to women's subordinate status in the labour market needs particular emphasis. It has been too easy for critics of EEO programs to refer to women's childcare responsibilities, or to their socialisation before their working lives, or to the choices they have made in education and employment when attempting to explain their lack of career advancement or lower rates of pay.

There is a further reason for concentrating on organisational processes. EEO plans are devised in acknowledgment that it is within work organisations that inequalities may be initiated or reinforced, through rules and practices that directly or indirectly discriminate against women. Yet EEO initiatives tend, in practice, to concentrate on strategies which might lead to a redistribution of women among existing job categories without questioning the distribution of tasks among jobs, or the relationships between jobs in different occupational categories. Neither do they promote close investigation of daily practices which use gender as the basis for decision-making.

We need to explore organisational arrangements by going beyond the assumption that a neutral administrative logic prevails or can be forged, and ask, to what extent do gender relationships inform the application of rules, hiring decisions, initial assignment practices, training and development decisions, promotional patterns, performance evaluation, salary offers and conditions of work?

It would appear, and illustrations are provided in this chapter to support this view, that ideas about masculinity and femininity are embedded in organisational arrangements and that the opportunity to accumulate 'merit' and the attribution of 'merit' are structured along gender lines. If we accept that merit, defined as job-related qualities of individuals, is reproduced and/or changed by organisational activity, then we must look closely at how this affects different categories of workers. It may be that perceptions of gender-based competencies and inclinations affect assignment and other practices and therefore the distribution of women and men among different types of opportunity structures within work organisations. It may be, too, that as EEO programs successfully eliminate discriminatory rules, discriminatory practices based on interpretations of such rules produce similar effects but go relatively unnoticed at an official level.

We need to emphasise the *social* nature of the gender relationships to which we refer. It is not possible to speak of the fortunes of individual women without reference to the structure of relationships between men and women in our society. Women, historically speaking, have not been as active or as successful as men in pursuing their work-related interests and neither have they had the same opportunities to do so collectively, through trade unions or professional associations. Whether it be 'coercive or cultural', it is unlikely that women 'will exploit the opportunities for bargaining presented by their working environments as intensively as do their ... male counterparts' (Ryan, 1981: 17). If organisational practices have been built up historically with men's typical life patterns as their foundation—including men's reliance, generally speaking, on domestic support—through a mobilisation of masculine bias, then reference to women in organisations is a reference to a general condition at the workplace, despite variations in women's experiences there. That is why we need to cast our investigative net to the structural arrangements which, if left intact, will continue to operate to the disadvantage of women in paid employment and which will be activated to re-create women's subordinate status.

A central question, if one is going to counter the ideology of individual choice in job and career decisions, is whether women are in positions within organisations because they choose to be there, or because there are allocative processes occurring which lead them to be appointed to or remain in positions where advancement opportunities are not readily available. This is clearly not a cut-and-dried matter, but I choose to emphasise the allocative processes because the evidence suggests that their impact is more significant than much of the writings on the subject would allow. Certainly different answers to this question underlie the arguments for and against affirmative action programs.

The concept of choice informs liberal political thought and neo-classical economic thought, and both are dominant modes of explanation of individuals' public activity. They inform the arguments of those who believe that affirmative actions are a new form of injustice, a form of positive discrimination. Those arguing in the tradition of liberal democratic thought find that the concern with 'abstract groups and their purported rights' violates that 'essence of liberalism [which] has always been concerned with the welfare, rights and responsibilities of *individuals qua individuals*' (Hawkesworth, 1984:340, citing Nisbet, 1977:52). On the other hand, proponents of affirmative action implicitly or explicitly question the adequacy of these theoretical formulations for explaining the distribution, indeed the generation of economic and other rewards in our society. They suggest that if individual members of a group are disadvantaged as a result of their group membership, then the structuring of opportunities in education and employment are neither neutral nor fair (Hawkesworth, 1984:43). Redress and positive measures, then need to be addressed to the group and to relationships between groups.

An exploration of the different conceptions of individuality underlying the opposing points of view gives us a clearer picture of what is being contested. Hawkesworth's discussion is particularly useful for our purposes here. She contrasts what she calls an atomistic conception of individuality with a socialised conception. The former 'asserts the primacy of choice and effort as determinants of individuals' success'; the latter emphasises the impact of cultural norms and group practices upon the development of individual identity (1984; 346, 336). She argues that the atomistic conception 'overlooks the extent to which the individual's impressions, desires, sensations and aspirations are socially constructed, founded upon a host of intersubjective understandings, incorporated into language, culture and tradition' (1984:345).

Those who base their propositions on the atomistic view are in effect asserting that organisational processes or labour market processes deal even-handedly with each individual party to the employment situation (Ryan, 1981:4). Orthodox economic theory is based on the atomistic conception of individuality. The human capital school, for instance, characterises 'an individual's productivity as almost entirely under that individual's control. He or she is born with certain capacities, develops them through training or education, 'chooses to invest' in himself or herself, and then presents the prospective employer with these capacities for appraisal and reward (Bergmann and Darity, 1980:156).

The socialised conception — that individuality is a product of historical processes, of racial, sexual or cultural experiences (Hawkesworth, 1984:336) — can be extended into organisational life. We can go beyond conventional explanations of an individual woman's employment opportunities and look at perceptions of her at the workplace which are consistent with wider social evaluations of women's work and which affect her initial job assignment and subsequent advancement.

But the socialised conception of individuality gives us another leverage point. It indicates that identity is in constant construction through social practices, including those at the workplace (Game and Pringle, 1983:16). The atomistic view gives a static picture of identity, and omits work organisations as a ground on which it develops. Furthermore, identity in the atomistic view is neither masculine nor feminine, but sexually undifferentiated (Pateman, 1983:10), whereas in the socialised view, masculinity and femininity are integral dimensions of the continuing process of individual identity formation.

The following examples of organisational processes provide evidence to challenge the atomistic conception of individuality on which opposition to affirmative action is firmly based and which 'influences [one's] very capacity to perceive the existence of discrimination' (Hawkesworth, 1984:336).

INITIAL JOB ASSIGNMENT

Initial job assignment discrimination gains its importance through the ways it feeds into other forms of discrimination, including wage discrimination (Newman, 1982: Rosenbaum, 1980; 1985).

A study was conducted into a New South Wales Government department to establish whether patterns of job assignment and subsequent advancement emerged within a cohort of base-level clerical recruits, all of whom came in under an identical entry standard. Areas with flat career structures 'attracted' more women; at the next level women were spread over fewer streams (despite an overall majority in numbers) and there were fewer female promotions above the second (MR, 1982). At base-grade level or during the year following, when decisions allocating people to areas of work are made, most recruits are not aware of the career implications or advancement opportunities in different clerical specialisations. The allocator may well know that a particular area is 'dead end' and this study suggests that women are more likely to be streamed in those directions. The women end up receiving what Rosenbaum (1979:237) calls a custodial socialisation rather than a challenging one, affecting self-assessment and others' assessment of capacity for advancement.

If we look further up, and ask why women are not entering higher grades, we need to look back at initial assignment and early decisions about streaming. If caution is exercised in allocating women to challenging positions, the problems are reinforced further up the hierarchy. The evidence suggests that initial assignment to challenging positions is more significant for subsequent advancement than later events, that 'assessment in an employee's first few years ha[s] profound and enduring effects on later career outcomes' (Rosenbaum, 1979:223: see also Berlew and Hall, 1966; Veiga, 1983). To the extent that choice is exercised, it is governed in large part by the ways the situation is structured by the allocation process, ways informed by sex of the recruit, but consisting of processes the atomistic conception of individuality does not provide for.

TRAINING, DEVELOPMENT AND STUDY LEAVE

We can distinguish training which enhances people's current job performance from that which is preparation for promotion. Indeed, this distinction may well be formalised in an organisation's procedures. But there remain areas where the distinction is blurred. Supervisors then interpret the circumstances according to their own views.

An investigation was carried out in a Commonwealth Government department of supervisors' comments on application forms filled in by candidates for the Study Assistance Scheme. The investigation explored the reasons given by supervisors for approving the applications for study leave of women and men in jobs which had no opportunities for advancement built into them (routine) and jobs from which people normally advanced to positions further up in the hierarchy (non-routine). The focus of the study was on whether the supervisor approved the application for short-term benefits only (that is, for improving current performance) or for long-term and more general benefits (that is, for career development). For men in non-routine jobs, 100 per cent of supervisors' comments focused on long-term benefits; for women in non-routine jobs 60 per cent; the supervisors of men in routine jobs focused on long-term career benefits in 91 per cent of the cases, and for women in 56 per cent of the cases (Major, 1985). Approval for study assistance, then, was given to more men in routine jobs on the basis of career development than to women in positions which allow for some advancement. Sex of the applicant was a more salient characteristic than organisational position.

This example indicates that the situation is not simply that people in routine jobs are assumed not to be capable of moving out of them: men and women are dealt with differently, whether they be in routine or non-routine jobs (see Kanter, 1980). Expectations of them are different. We have already noted the importance of expectations as determinants of behaviour and aspirations. There is no possibility of reconciling these practices with the atomistic formulation of individuality which denies the force of social cues (Rosenbaum, 1979:225), of others' expectations, and of the limitations others impose on one's career prospects.

'TRYING HELPS MEN, HURTS WOMEN'

This example relates to *perceptions* of ability or competence. Effort — individuals' efforts to improve themselves — is significant for productivity and therefore advancement and wages, in orthodox economic thinking. However, we can criticise the gender-blindness of this framework by referring to research results which indicate that the perception of effort, and the interpretation of it, are different when viewed in men and women, with subsequent effects on reward structures.

Sex stereotyping has been shown to affect the evaluation of people's performance on tasks and the attribution of causes of good and poor performance. Men *and* women tend to rate men's work more highly than women's, and men's performance on tasks more highly than women's identical performance (Nieva and Gutek, 1980; O'Leary and Hansen, 1982; Ruble et al., 1984; Shepela and Viviano, 1984). When the participants in experimental studies are asked to give explanations for successful performance on the part of men and women, they tend to rate the female as more motivated and less able than the male. In other words, good female performance is perceived as due to effort, and good male performance as due to ability:

> The process of evaluation includes not only the judgement of the worth of the performance being evaluated but also the attribution of causality for that performance. Causal attributions are important because they determine whether specific performances are seen as accidental occurrences or as likely to be consistently repeatable in the future. (Nieva and Gutek, 1980:269)

If, for instance, successful performance is attributed to ability, then one would suppose that the level of performance might be repeated for some time to come. This is relevant to decisions about advancement (Ruble et al., 1984:351). If, on the other hand, the performance is due to effort, then this could be regarded as a temporary or situationally determined event, leading to no firm conclusion about future performance. O'Leary and Hansen conclude from their review of various research findings that 'trying helps men, hurts women': effort is 'perceived as diagnostic of men's ability, and compensatory of women's lack thereof' (1982:117).

JOB DESIGN AND THE POLITICS OF SKILL

Many jobs have been designed on a gender base. By this is not meant simply that we can describe typical men's jobs and typical women's jobs, or that we can identify features of jobs that might make them more appropriate for one sex or the other. While we do need to investigate how some have been designed in such a way that being a man or being a woman is viewed as fundamental to their perform-ance, we have to understand that as a reflection of gender *relation-ships*. Cockburn, for example, in reference to the design of work in some typically masculine trades, comments that 'units of work . . . are political in their design . . . The appropriation of bodily effectivity on the one hand and the design of machinery and processes on the other have often converged in such a way as to constitute men as capable and women as inadequate' (1981:51).

Secretarial and 'boss' jobs are probably the clearest expressions of work that developed and became structured into organisations that used gender relationships as their basis. Characteristics regarded as typically feminine — notably, dependence and lack of ambition for oneself — are the complement of the masculine characteristics of the incumbent boss, to whom the secretary is attached. The perception of the job incumbent — the female secretary — informs the job definition. The definition of the main components of the job stress the relation-ship of it to another job. This definition is used for the evaluation of performance; the job is selectively perceived as a 'circumscribed "helping" role' (Schrank and Riley, 1976:94); performance is assessed in terms of effectiveness in assisting a higher-ranking incumbent. What is not assessed, because it is perceived as unimportant, are the skills which actually equip the incumbent to assume a higher-ranking job herself.

The skills valued, then, are the skills in looking after the interests of another job incumbent. This has wide-reaching effects on the opportunities offered to secretaries:

> Many female jobs 'tied' to higher ranked male jobs would pro-bably provide superb training experience for upward mobility. It is a commonplace observation that many women, especially secre-taries, actually perform many of the tasks that constitute the asso-ciated male job. Such women are brought into decision-making and they exercise control over the male incumbent's subordinates. If one were to construct a training job that would allow the trainee to see and participate in the work of a higher ranking office, the design in many respects might resemble the secretarial job. (Schrank and Riley, 1976:93—94)

The determination of the relative worth of jobs, then, at present reflects a masculine bias and undermines the training and experience that much of women's work involves. Many examples of this can be presented. A general condition for this situation is the combination of three factors: the higher value placed on masculine work; the fact that even when women's skills have been acquired through training and experience they have been explained partly in terms of 'natural' ability; and the lack of recognition of the informal training ground that the domestic sphere provides for many of the skills for which women are employed (see Burton, 1985:126). For example, the job evaluator for the US Government Printing Office 'awarded no points to female bindery workers for training or experience in hand sewing "because the sewing was of the variety that most women know how to perform" thereby undervaluing the female compared to the male book-binder jobs' (Ferraro, 1984:1170). The male counterpart was paid more for doing the same job because he had to acquire the skills. However, the masculine equivalent of 'natural' ability is highly rewarded at the workplace, as witnessed by the remuneration paid for many jobs demanding physical effort.

We can extend this view even further by taking account of the fluidity of the category of skill or merit. Definitions of what is meritorious can undergo change depending on the power of particular groups to define it. Phillips and Taylor remark that skill is a direct correlate of the sex and power of those defining it, an ideological category rather than an objective economic fact (1980:79). Kessler and associates suggest that 'women pursuing expertise may find it being redefined as they reach for it' (1985:46). This partly results from the process already referred to: women's successful performance is less likely to be attributed to ability than men's successful performance. We have, too, to take into account the likelihood that if jobs can be filled by women, they will come to be perceived as less difficult.

THE EXERCISE OF AUTHORITY

The examples of allocations to and remunerations for positions where the exercise of authority is important illustrate a number of practices which together contribute to the unequal fortunes of women and men within work organisations. The cultural association of masculinity and authority (Caplow, 1954:238–41) is reproduced through the decisions made by managers and supervisors who are concerned, for productivity reasons, not to disturb this 'natural' relationship. Arguments are put forward about women's incapacity to perform in supervisory positions, not because of a lack of competence, but because of the effect it would have on groups of workers, and therefore on productivity levels. 'If one person is assigned to supervise a group of employees, the supervisor will be more effective in expediting production if the supervisor has no personal charact-eristics that make it difficult for some of the assigned subordinates to give respect and to submit to direction' (Bergmann and Darity, 1980:157).

In other words, the 'taste for discrimination' can be justified in productivity terms. Here productivity is acknowledged to be a function of a group's relationships and not simply a function of individual effort. This example reinforces the argument I began with: the relationships between motivation, aspiration, effort and oppor-tunity are not located within an individual but are a function of relationships between individuals. The chances of a person to acquire and demonstrate 'merit' are heavily dependent on the content and quality of the social relations of the workplace.

This example, too, needs to be put into the social context as a whole, where the exercise of authority is highly regarded and re-warded. Level of remuneration is a concrete and visible symbol of authority (Rosenbaum, 1980:2); see also Greenwood, 1984), and of the hierarchy within organisations. Indeed, the association of high salary with authority legitimates the hierarchy. The allocation of women to 'complex staff positions that involve significant discretion' and of men to positions 'involving considerable supervisory authority and control of major assets' (Sigelman et al., 1982:668), the latter being defined as being of greater value to the organisation, simul-taneously legitimates the relative status positions of men and women and their income differential.

CONCLUSION

Current practices do not wholly rest on individual merit or com-petence but on perceptions, evaluations and decisions already based on a set of arrangements and understandings which provide women with less access to opportunities than men. Analyses of the distri-bution of opportunities as determined by daily practices could be carried out by setting up careful monitoring devices directed at prac-tices which research such as that detailed above brings to light. These might add to our understanding of the ways in which people are favoured because they are *perceived* to be more capable, or more deserving, of advancement, on grounds other than those of job competency.

The illustrations provided above highlight the ways in which social processes enter organisations through perceptual and cognitive maps which emphasise gender as one of the more significant guideposts for interpreting organisational behaviour. They served as a warning to those who seek to teach women simply to 'fit in' to existing organisational arrangements. These are not experienced by men and women in the same way. Behaviours important for men's success are not directly transferable to women because identical behaviour is not perceived or treated in the same way. Success is not defined in sex-neutral terms.

The implementation of EEO programs tends to concentrate on the distribution of opportunities in organisations, opportunities for certain jobs, promotion, financial rewards, training and development, and mobility. It tends, too, to concentrate on who has what job, and what women must learn to compete effectively for existing jobs. This concentration is at the expense of a critical examination of the current shape of the opportunity structures within organisations and the activities which tend to reproduce it.

To attempt to dismantle indirectly discriminatory rules as if they are a relic from the past, as if their removal will effectively eliminate the problem of discrimination, is to deny that their presence has continued to structure the interests and perceptions of current organisational participants. The attempt to remove them will generate a new field of protective activity, in the practical application of the now non-discriminatory rules. The mobilisation of masculine bias does not disappear with the elimination of discriminatory rules; it is to practices that we must turn our attention, as well. When we refer to equitable organisational arrangements, we are not restricting our view to the 'narrow, distributive concerns of equity' (Pateman, 1981:36) which address who has what job, nor to the formal rules governing the allocation process, but to the exercise of power at the workplace, how jobs are organised and practised and the fundamental preconditions for the development of alternative arrangements.

EEO programs have the potential to take account of the bases of inequality which are not captured by the atomistic conception of individuality. The concept of 'disparate impact' embodied in EEO programs shifts the emphasis from the process of distribution of employment opportunity, and the role individual choice plays in that distribution, to the processes whereby opportunities are generated, structured and allocated in ways which perpetuate the dominance of masculine values and priorities.

EEO practitioners are in a position to work towards shifting the ground rules so that it is harder to mobilise a masculine bias in a wide range of decision-making processes, and easier for EEO advocates to apply in practice the principles they believe to be fair. A case in point is some guidelines for selection processes developed recently by a small working party set up by the Australian Public

Service Board. The recommendations arising out of the working party's deliberations included one which attempted to get a grip on an apparent paradox of EEO practice: the more attempts are made to eliminate subjectivity from decision-making, the more rigid became the criteria on which decisions were made, thus excluding from consideration valuable options, or, in this case, applicants with relevant qualities or experiences not considered when the criteria were set up. The working party recommended that, rather than determining a priori the qualities and experiences relevant to the performance in the job, the selection criteria could be framed in relation to job outcomes, and applicants asked to demonstrate the suitability of their qualifications and experiences for performance directed to those outcomes. In this way, experiences in apparently dissimilar contexts could be brought to the attention of the selectors, and experiences previously regarded as 'unsuitable' would not be ruled out of consideration.

This is an example of how a formal rule change can affect the likelihood of particular outcomes, and minimise the possibility of particular biases systematically being applied in decision-making. The research findings dealt with above provide examples of areas where formal rule changes might also affect potential outcomes in particular ways, giving EEO advocates a greater likelihood of achieving their aims. Further research of this kind, of course, needs to be carried out to inform strategy development.

An organisational focus on how gender operates as a central structuring principle at the workplace draws attention to the dynamics of the relationships among job-holders and thus captures a dimension of the position of women workers not highlighted by the more conventional industry and occupational analyses of gender at work. The understanding of discrimination and inequality within work organisations might be furthered by exploring the historically structured links between perceptions and evaluations of individual 'merit' on the one hand and gender relationships on the other.

3 Can equal employment opportunity prevail?

Affirmative action and equal employment opportunity programs aim to eliminate discriminatory employment practices and to promote equal employment opportunities for women. In practice, this is usually understood to mean that the merit principle forms the basis for appointment to positions and for promotions.

'Merit' is rarely defined. More often than not, attempts to define it emphasise what it is not, such as a person's sex, race, marital status as grounds for appointment, or other criteria unrelated to job performance. The concept of merit refers to a *relationship* between a person's qualifications and those required for performance in particular positions.

EEO legislation in Australia has prompted attempts to define merit-based selection procedures. For example, the main Australian Public Service legislation on this point lays down (*Public Service Reform Act* 1984, section 33, sub-section 1) that where an appointment to the [Public] Service is to be made:

(a) all persons who are eligible for appointment to the Service have, so far as is practicable, a reasonable opportunity to apply for the appointment; and

(b) the appointment is made on the basis of an assessment of the relative suitability of the applicants for the appointment, having regard to:

　　(i) the nature of the duties to be performed by the person appointed; and

　　(ii) the abilities, qualifications, experience and other attributes of each applicant that are relevant to the performance of those duties.

Equal Employment Opportunity is a policy that all personnel activities will be conducted so as to ensure that, for each vacancy in an organisation, people with equal probability of job success have equal probability of being hired for or promoted to the job. In other words, a person's ... sex ... should not reduce her or his chances of employment or promotion. (Ziller, 1980:13)

Of course, the determination of the best person for the job is made with reference to factors over and above the skill and knowledge requirements for performance in a position, as the phrase 'and other attributes' above implies. A number of qualities might be desirable in an occupant for a position. It would also appear that selections on merit rarely occur without reference to 'organisational and institutional interests' (Cohen and Pfeffer, 1986:2).

This means that judgments are being exercised, that subjective assessments of relative suitability are being made. The merit principle is, one might say, the 'black box' of the EEO process, the key to its functioning. Merit is hard to define and many elements can be introduced into it which run counter to EEO principles as we understand them. Such factors as willingness to relocate and other 'business-related' requirements can be and are used as indicators of merit.

Definitions of direct and indirect discrimination are set out in the *Sex Discrimination Act* 1984 and in State anti-discrimination legislation (see Ronalds, 1987:96–101). The two terms mean the same as the terms used in the U.S.A: 'disparate treatment' and 'disparate impact'. Yet, despite legislative initiatives introducing the concept of indirect discrimination, the 'soft' understanding of this prevails in organisations and includes such initiatives as removing rules which can be demonstrated to be unnecessary (such as the height ruling for police officers) or those work practices which reflect union strength (such as a seniority rule), providing safety signs in several languages, and providing the type of affirmative actions, such as assertiveness training for women and English language classes for people of non-English-speaking backgrounds, to enable these people to catch up with the prevailing standard.

Rarely are policy-makers or senior managers heard to argue forcefully for the harder version, which includes a reassessment of the qualities which are to be sought and the relative pay rates which would be allocated to them, the various ways organisations can achieve effective performances, the need to reformulate corporate values, and the need to deal actively with the historical effects of past practices.

The 'politics of skill' is a phrase which draws attention to the power relationships governing the determination of appropriate qualifications for positions, to the question of whether some qualities, essential for performance in a job, are going to be acknowledged at all, and if they are, whether they are going to be paid for and at what rate. 'Comparable worth' or pay equity strategies have developed to deal with the apparent fact that many women's skills, drawn on by employers, are not remunerated at the rate of men's equivalent skills. Some of these skills appear to be regarded by employers as 'natural' female attributes rather than skills developed through training and experience, and are not perceived as requiring compensation (e.g. manual dexterity, social skills, caring qualities). Hearn and Parkin (1987:11) and Crompton and Jones (1984:146−47) discuss the undervaluing of 'domestic' work in organisations, for example, while Burton, Hag and Thompson (1987) review the literature dealing with the pay equity issue, with particular reference to Australian studies in this specific area.

Another issue of relevance is the question of the social construction of skilled work as a category distinct from unskilled work, and the political nature of much that is incorporated in the idea of a 'skilled performance' (see Manwaring and Wood, 1985:189), both issues being relevant to women's work in paid employment and dealt with extensively in the literature (see Cockburn, 1983; 1985; 1986; also Phillips and Taylor, 1980; Pollert, 1981; Cavendish, 1982). Bennett (1984), for example, examines the association of skilled work with men and unskilled work with women in the Australian industrial context. Attwood and Hatton (1983) discuss the ambiguous occupational status of hairdressing (unskilled work or craft?) and Game and Pringle (1983) discuss the gender base of skill definitions (see also O' Donnell, 1984 and Connell, 1987:99−106).

A person's relative 'merit' in relation to a vacant position or a promotional position is commonly understood to be based on their ability, or their capacity (which might include their potential), to perform in the position. But research evidence suggests that men are seen as being more able, as having more natural ability, in many areas, than women, or more of the important *kinds* of ability (see Ruble et al., 1984; O'Leary and Hansen, 1982). This is a form of stereotyping resulting, in the main, from attitudes and practices which are based on the idea that women are better at emotional work such as that required in looking after children, and men at hard physical work or hard mental work, such as that involved in particular jobs in the paid workforce. The result is that when men and women perform identically on particular tasks, their performances are perceived differently (see Shepela and Viviano, 1984; McArthur, 1985).

Furthermore, ability is notoriously difficult to define, identify and measure. So we tend to use indicators of it, and education and work experience have been significant here. But something else is too. People's job history appears to be used by selectors as a significant indicator of ability. This means, in particular, that the paths taken through an organisation or occupation and the time taken to get to a particular position are important for assessments of a person's ability, or capacity for further advancement. Rosenbaum (1979, 1984) clearly indicates how these processes affect women's advancement rates within organisations (see also Miller, 1986).

These processes can be applied to a clerk-typist in an organisation to illustrate the likely effects on women workers. We can put together the two processes of women being perceived as less able than men and the effect of job history on perceptions of a person's capacity to advance, and add to them another, the application of what is called 'availability bias' (McArthur, 1985:55). This refers to the ways in which the information that is readily available about a person — that she can type, for example — overwhelms the other information that might be gained about the rest of the work she performs, which might include activities of a clerical or administrative nature. This means that the assessment of her potential to advance into other areas of work is based on only a segment of what she has demonstrated she can achieve.

It raises the related issue of whether many jobs, apart from any clear-cut technical skills or knowledge base that might be required to perform in them, are so static, so immune to the shaping effects of different incumbents, that one is able to compare two competent candidates for a position and deem one more suitable than the other.

THE BELIEF IN THE OBJECTIVE EXISTENCE OF JOBS

The emphasis on redistributing people among existing jobs as if these are neutral and fixed entities has a limited effectiveness while jobs are designed on a gender base, while the sex of the typical occupants affects the design of the job, the nature of its content, the perception of its demands and its relationships with other jobs.

Davies and Rosser (1986) discuss how gender is 'written in' to jobs, and give a particular illustration of this in the job of the female office manager:

> A gendered job occurs where its unacknowledged informal responsibilities extend well beyond what the formal grading structure could demand, and are elaborated in a way that is dependent upon the gender and life-cycle stage of the job holder (see also Knights and Willmott, 1986:8, Kelley, 1984 and Schrank and Riley, 1976).

27

As Anselme and Weisz (1985:39) put it:

> A bad job refers not just to the technical characteristics of the job held but also to the professional and social position of the holder, and thus to the social characteristics of the job itself.

When we refer to the sex-segregated nature of the labour market, and set up strategies to disperse women across a greater number of industry and occupational classifications, we need to take into account the active shaping and redefining of jobs that goes on in the organisation in response to the typical sex of the occupants. It may be, for example, that our statistical data on the increase in women in management jobs is misleading. Lyle and Ross (1973:8) point to the ways in which, when management positions are '"turned over" to women [they are placed at] a lower position on the firm's corporate organisation chart and with a lower range of salary levels'.

In *Women's Worth* (Burton et al., 1987 esp. Ch. 5) very different descriptions of similar jobs and identical functions were looked at, descriptions which partly relied on the sex of the typical or actual occupants. For example, when contact with other organisations was a feature of the job, the description of the work was quite different for men's and women's jobs. Men's jobs were described as 'fostering and promoting a good image' for the organisation, 'maintaining good commercial relationships with suppliers', while descriptions of women's jobs included such phrases as 'the incumbent must show good judgment when purchasing food items', and 'must have a good telephone manner'. The job title of secretary frequently led to an evaluation of the position which took no account of the clerical and administrative work performed by the incumbents. The definition of a job has implications not only for the current evaluation of the job, but also for the assessment of the occupant's potential for advancement.

Even the geographic location of work is partly governed by notions of appropriate incumbents. Here we can see contradictory effects on potential employees of an organisation's decision to relocate some of its work. Efforts which appear on the surface to open up equal opportunities can in fact be closing off the very options that need to be provided under EEO programs. Companies and government departments which move some of their activities to working-class suburbs are offering greater employment opportunities to people from working-class families in the region. But they offer different opportunities for men and women in these areas.

Some firms and departments are relocating white-collar work that is design for and offered to young women with the School Certificate and young men with the Higher School Certificate (on the grounds that the young men will move through the ranks along a career path and the young women will perform the routine clerical work for a few years before they leave to have a family) (see Collinson and Knights, 1986:153; Ashridge Management College, 1980:31). Some of the jobs on offer have been designed for young women with fewer years of education, and others have been designed (particularly to be performed part-time) for married women with some earlier, relevant, workforce experience.

A manager in a private sector firm, speaking to me of the redesign of jobs and the associated removal of career paths when some data input work was taken out of the firm's branches and centralised in a working-class suburb, reported that he would not consider placing young men in those positions. These job redesign and locational decisions and their gender base have been amply documented in the literature (see Kelley, 1984:264; Maguire 1986).

Some office jobs are designed for high turnover, and/or for a layer of workers who will not demand careers and advancement opportunities, so that limited opportunities are provided to those who do expect them, and who might otherwise leave for better positions elsewhere (Crompton and Jones (1984:162)). There is little evidence that the situation described in the following (Heritage, 1983:133) does not still apply:

> During the 1960s the differential recruitment of men and women [into banks] followed a pattern in which women were recruited in direct proportion to the rapidly rising volume of routine work, while men were employed in proportion to the much slower growth in the numbers of bank branches which they would eventually command.

The business practice of opening career development opportunities for young men at the expense of those for young women, reinforces dependency relationships within the very households that are apparently being served by these decisions.

In other words, these practices re-create the sexual division of labour in the family. Men and women from the same family background are entering organisations on a different footing, reinforcing the financial advantage men have within the family, the greater bargaining power they have in the matter of job transfers, and the greater likelihood that the women will, indeed, leave work to raise the children that both they and their partners desire. As one author put it, 'The labour market operates as it does partly because of the choices and preferences and definitions of the situation of the actors involved, but these in part reflect experience of the way it operates' (Brown, 1984:72).

THE MYTH OF RATIONAL ORGANISATION

The organisational response to EEO legislation and guidelines conforms to the models of organisations as rational, instrumental entities rather than to the reality of the political processes that make up organisational life. The response reflects the view that 'the provision of equal opportunity can largely be guaranteed simply by the introduction of certain employment procedures ... Equal opportunity is defined as a technical problem, for which technical solutions are appropriate: monitoring systems, more "rational" selection criteria, "best practice" in general' (Jenkins, 1987:118; see also Heydebrand, 1983:97).

This view relies on the myths of bureaucracies as consisting of rule-bound behaviour, of the value-freedom of the administration of policy, of the automatic development, from broad policy guidelines, of efficient practices and procedures. It denies the politics of rule use, the power of custom, the scope for interpreting the meaning of events in different ways. It denies the fact that rules are organisational-political resources, and people have different capacities to use them as such. Organisations are political entities; they are constituted by activities which represent competing values, conflicting interests, competition over scarce resources and the exercise of power. The relatively powerless EEO coordinators, for example, in order to render EEO palatable to those with the power to ensure its success enter the terrain of the defenders of rational models of organisations. They are caught up in a contradictory situation: denying the place of social values in organisations and the marketplace while needing to highlight their existence; emphasising administrative solutions to organisational problems while needing to highlight the social and political dimensions of organisational life.

From whose point of view, then, is organisational decision-making rational? The following comment from a young woman in response to the question 'how would you change the bank if you were in charge?' would appear to support a corporate philosophy which emphasises service to customers and the provision of interesting work for its employees. She says:

> In my department they have each person doing a different job. One girl will do all the important business, one will do letters of credit, and so on. I think it would be better if they separated the work by client company. That way you'd be doing different things, which is interesting. You should learn all of it. And if you're doing the same company, you become familiar with the way they like to settle things, and you'd be calling them up all the time and getting to know them. (Tepperman, 1976:17)

This respondent added that if she ran the bank, she would distribute the more interesting work (at the time performed by male collectors and note tellers) among the women as well.

Management rationality is in direct conflict with that of this young woman, who would enlarge jobs and make them more meaningful and enhance customer satisfaction at the same time. It is in direct conflict with the aim of EEO programs, which is to enhance the employment opportunities of women relative to those of men. It is in direct conflict with the general aim of encouraging young women to alter their perceptions of their place in the world of paid work.

As Thompson (1982:57) remarks, 'most of the time most people behave rationally. That is, they strive quite successfully to make as much sense as they can of where they find themselves'. Connell (1983:156) deals with the apparently irrational (certainly unintended) effects of rational behaviour through the concept of 'praxis traps': 'where people do things for good reasons and skilfully, in situations that turn out to make their original purpose impossible to achieve'. But powerful groups can use rational discourse strategically and for legitimation (Brown, 1978).

Public and private sector firms are contributing to the very *behaviour* of women, which leads to their being denied advancement opportunities. As long as young women are placed in the more routine of jobs on offer which provide little in the way of challenge or self-esteem, the rational response is to look elsewhere for fulfilment and satisfaction.

ORGANISATIONAL CULTURES

Ouchi and Wilkins (1985:469) remark that 'perhaps it is through culture, rather than formal structure, that large firms can be bent to the will of their masters, and rendered predictable, "rational"'. The notion of an organisational culture, say Van Maanen and Barley (1985:40), 'has attained a faddish appeal in the business literature'. It can be used quite coercively to restrain an EEO officer who displays enthusiasm for altering customary ways of doing things. The culture of the organisation is presented as an almost sacred core of the company's identity and its uniqueness as something which gives the company its competitive edge. It is also presented as a coherent and neutral entity, as if it were possible for it to contain only one set of values and beliefs, to which everyone can equally subscribe. It is also presented as if it were not *constituted* by power relationships, but rather something which expresses the general interests and orientation of the organisation which are at the same time necessarily the shared interests and orientation of its participants.

This is a very conservative view, of course, denying the dynamic nature of any system of values and beliefs, and denying the need for the very thing the concept was designed to promote: the need for the organisation to adapt flexibly to changing social and economic circumstances.

Internally appointed EEO coordinators have a particularly difficult job. If they challenge the values, the rules, the practices, they are appearing disloyal. They are saying, in effect, I accepted your rules when I came here, but now I am the EEO coordinator I am changing my view and am criticising policies which I led you to believe I accepted, and indeed I probably got this position, as a senior female officer, because of my demonstrated loyalty to the organisation's way of doing things. This prompts a more general comment on the uncomfortable situation of the EEO co-ordinator in large organisations. Generally speaking, the people appointed to deal with EEO programs on a daily basis are appointed at middle management level. They report to a senior executive responsible for the EEO or AA management plan. This person may or may not have the view that EEO is an important organisational or employment issue. The EEO coordinator is left with the management of the program, with little real influence or power to have it implemented effectively.

When we refer to organisational cultures we are, by and large, talking about masculine cultures—values, preferred ways of doing things, ideas about appropriate work for men and women, based on ideas about men's role in paid work and women's role in the family. The view that masculinity is embedded in organisational structures is strongly supported by Ferguson (1984) and Eisenstein (1985). Within work organisations, ways of perceiving and interpreting events are structured around these associations of women with the domestic sphere and men with the sphere of public activity. Organisational cultures reflect women's marginal place within them; they reflect men's interests and the general situation of men in our society rather than the range of preferences and values held by women or the typical life circumstances of women who are entering organisations in greater numbers (see Buono and Kamm, 1983; Marshall, 1984).

As trivial as the following examples might appear (but see Goffman, 1979:6 for the impact of the cumulative burden of organisational trivialities), they provide evidence of the privileged position that masculine symbols, images and interests hold in everyday organisational life. It has been said many times that a photograph of a male manager's family on his desk is viewed with approval, as an indication of his stability and commitment to traditional values, whereas a photograph of a female manager's family is cause for concern and might indicate that her mind is not on her career. A collection of sporting gear in the corner of an office is acceptable: it symbolises activity and competitiveness. But one female manager was asked to remove the teapot from her desk; this is a domestic symbol, a strongly female one, and it causes discomfort (even though people drink tea in organisations).

In other words, the symbols and values of work organisations are decidedly non-domestic, and the same object—a family photograph—is perceived differently, depending on whether it is viewed through the filter of 'men at work' or 'women at work', because these filters lead to quite different ways of seeing the same objects or events. Men belong in the public world, and the photograph on the desk poses no danger to his position there. Indeed, the family is evidence of domestic support for male managers. The photograph on the woman's desk is a reminder of her marginal place at work and of the dangers associated with too close an association with the intimate and emotional, the non-rational relationships domestic life involves.

To fit in, woman have to take on some of the values and preferred ways of doing things in work organisations, which are grounded in men's, not women's experiences. Morgan (1986:179—80) reveals the 'impression management' that is required of women in organisations and the greater effort women need to put into 'accomplishing everyday reality' in male-dominated organisational contexts. It means, too, that the qualities women bring to organisations, whether or not they are drawn on in the work of the enterprise, are less likely to be valued there, because to accord them their proper place, their actual value, would undermine the myth of the organisation as a rational, instrumental, public, impersonal domain and it would raise the awkward possibility of the domestic sphere being a training ground for qualities and skills demanded by work organisations.

Critics of EEO within organisations argue that the problem of women's participation in the workforce has to be resolved within educational institutions and the family, and while they are right to emphasise educational and family practices, they are at the same time passing the responsibility on to other institutions. Within government schools in many parts of Australia girls and boys are playing sports together, and there is active encouragement of girls into maths and science. Students of both sexes take the classes which used to be streamed along gender lines (home economics, technical drawing and so on). In some schools science is being taught in a segregated class because of a concern with the negative effects on young women of learning about science alongside their male peers.

Yet these same young people enter work organisations to discover that the 'real world' conducts its business on the assumption that there is women's work, and there is men's work. In banks, for example, only women are put on to proof machines and routine data input work (Game and Pringle, 1983). In a workplace I visited, a young man recently recruited expressed a regret that there were not more women in the section, as he had looked forward to friendships with both men and women on entering employment.

In these and other ways, organisational practices actively undermine the considerable achievements that have been made in the public education system (although I am not suggesting for a minute that this is an equal opportunity arena). Organisations are central sites of socialisation; they themselves contribute to the social construction of gender relations, of ideas about masculinity and femininity, and to the more general social subordination of women.

As Game and Pringle (1983:16–17) put it, when they set out the main argument of their book: 'gender is constantly renegotiated and recreated ... [gender] identities are constructed through social practices such as work'. Connell, on the social production of gender relations, which occurs within the household, at school, at work, at play, argues (1983:42):

> Gender categories, in social interaction as well as ideology, are composite, constructed. They, and the relation between them, reflect the balance of forces in a complex generative process that is rich in possibilities of dislocation, contradiction and crisis.

EEO AND ORGANISATIONAL CHANGE

There is a general tendency in public and private sector organisations to devolve personnel activity onto regional offices and company branches (see Chapter 5 The case for a central EEO agency in the Australian Public Service). Accompanying this is the move to 'mainstream' EEO, to give line managers the responsibility for implementing the policy. At the same time, organisational change processes — the introduction of new information and other technologies, the development of flatter hierarchies, work reorganisation, location decisions — are occurring which actively undermine EEO progress. Changes are not planned to ensure equitable employment outcomes. EEO programs do not have an organisational auditing function, so that organisational changes are unlikely to be negotiated around a strong EEO perspective. EEO personnel are not powerful enough to influence these processes, and, to date, unions have not shown an interest in incorporating such matters into their agreements, in the way they frequently have for the introduction of new technologies.

By not accounting for issues of indirect or systemic discrimination, these changes reinforce the sex-segregated nature of the labour market. The rational models of organisations present a picture of a hierarchical structure which allows for the coordination of specialist activity, and the allocation of people to positions on the basis of their skills and aptitudes in such a way that the work is performed in the most efficient and effective way, in line with corporate goals. So a move towards flatter hierarchies or the introduction of new information technologies are presented as being in the general interests of the company (or agency) in terms of efficiency or productivity. This may or may not, depending on certain other factors, have a negative effect on employment opportunities overall.

What is not addressed here is the differential effect on men and women, depending on the jobs they hold in different internal labour markets within the organisation (developed through rules and customs around recruitment, wage-setting, promotion, transfer, training and so on). Indeed Rosenbaum (1984:209) observes that the gender allocation practices in organisations are so ingrained in job definitions and job evaluations that they seem to be part of the fixed organisational structure. If the *gender structuring* of organisations is not taken into account in the implementation of these changes — that is, the ways gender shapes the form and character of internal labour markets, the ways men and women are allocated to different internal labour markets, the differential treatment they receive within them, and the differential effects of experience of them on aspirations and opportunities — women will continue to be systematically disadvantaged. Further evidence of sex segregation within internal labour markets is provided by Hartmann (1987) and Kelley (1987).

As Osterman (1984:165) points out, 'formal and informal rules concerning job definition and reassignments shape the configuration of a technical innovation and also the consequences for the labor force'. In the case of the introduction of new information technologies the most repetitive of clerical labour will be transformed, and here we are referring, in the main, to women's jobs. An effective EEO program would mean positive action to ensure not only that the new jobs are designed to be more meaningful than simple data input, but also that women have access to the more interesting jobs that such technologies have the potential to create. But what public or private sector management group has expressed a commitment to EEO in this context, and has developed a strategy to ensure that the results do not further disadvantage women?

In the case of flatter structures and work reorganisation, we have a clear example of the importance of taking into account organisational processes over time. Women have traditionally worked within flat structures. Just as EEO is providing the impetus to move women into higher positions, supervisory and lower management jobs are becoming scarcer. And unless we are careful with strategies to integrate keyboard into clerical and administrative work, we will end up encouraging women into work which is becoming more routine and with fewer real opportunities for advancement, such as the segments of customer service work which are becoming computerised and less challenging. This is a real issue, at present, as the integration of keyboard work into clerical and administrative structures is a strategy currently being implemented within the APS and as State public sector organisations open up advancement opportunities for keyboard workers.

Women in these positions have little power to define the new situation and to make claims on the more interesting work that is created. Again, without active EEO strategies to shape the process of work allocation, even the more interesting keyboard work will be taken up by male clerical rather than by female keyboard officers.

Such phenomena as 'tipping' (men leaving a job area because women are entering it) and Cleverley's 'fear of contagious effeminacy' (see chapter 1) raise massive problems for the future efficacy of EEO programs. How will non-gender-based allocation of jobs in any work-restructuring, job-redesign exercise occur? When we talk about moving women into areas where men predominate, are we also talking about moving men into areas where females predominate, such as in data input, secretarial support work, receptionist and telephonist work? Or will all these jobs have to change, have their gender base dismantled, before a general dispersion of women and men among jobs will occur? And what might be the preconditions for this?

Equity strategies directed at women's employment must challenge, at one and the same time, the twin ideas of women's place and women's worth by tackling the occupational and hierarchical distribution of women *and* and generally low social value placed on women and the work they perform.

PART II
EEO in Practice in the Australian Public Service

4 Towards a redefinition of merit

At an EEO Conference in Sydney in 1984 Peter Wilenski (1984:16) threw out a challenge to academics like myself who have written papers criticising traditional applications of the merit principle or the ways in which suitability for positions has been defined within the public service. He felt we had to go beyond criticism and involve ourselves in discussion as to what the practical implications of our comments might be. He set up a small working party and a draft report, *Review of the Operation of the Merit Principle*, (Walden and Rosso, 1985) was prepared by officers at the Public Service Board.

Having participated in the working party, I then presented a seminar paper to the senior administrators at the Australian Public Service (APS) Board in February 1985 addressing this draft report. It never reached a final form. But it raises issues which I hope will not readily slip off an agenda for public administration reform.

The Public Service Board's corporate goal at the time was 'to promote in the Australian Public Service efficiency, responsiveness, equity and innovation in the development and implementation of government policies and programmes'. EEO policy contributed to this goal, through its emphasis on the recruitment and promotion of a diverse range of people. One of the EEO program's central aims is to reduce the tendency to recruit or advance people on the basis of their similarity to the selectors and/or to the characteristics and styles of the dominant groups in the organisation.

I felt that in order to address the draft report and speak about it to a group of senior administrators, I needed to discover what some of the public administration literature had to say about diversity and equity or, in their terms, the relationship between representative bureaucracies and administrative outcomes. I began seeking out some of the New Public Administration literature that had emerged from the United States in the late 1960s and 1970s which had an explicit concern with equity issues. The New Public Administration has been described as the administrative counterpart to the New Left, but could just as readily be described as the administrative absorption of the New Left. It certainly appears to have been a response to the possibility of major social conflict emerging in answer to governmental programs which appeared to exacerbate particular social and political crises — war, poverty and racism. There is a wide range of views expressed within this literature, but it is worth addressing here, since it sought 'to raise equity to the same level as efficiency and economy as a value in the practice of public administration' (Wilenski, 1984:8 see also Wilenski, 1986).

I found some recurring themes in the literature which could be related to the concerns expressed in the draft report. Some of them are directed to proposals for industrial democracy as a contribution to a participatory bureaucracy — representation was dealt with by the advocacy of more involvement of the existing workforce in decision-making. Although this is a different issue from that of recruiting a more diverse workforce, some of the comments made reflect what might well have been said had the writers contemplated such a move. There are several arguments that need addressing in the light of the recommendations of the report:

1 *That representativeness would be appropriate if it contributed to efficiency and productivity.* First, it is feared that diversity will bring undue conflict and dissension into the bureaucracy, thus undermining its efficient operation. Second, there is a belief that it might be incompatible with the principles of political democracy. In this view, the distinction between the political representative and the administrator must be preserved. The combination of these factors — time-consuming negotiation between different interests and the experimentation with different managerial processes — leads to the question of whether this is in the 'public interest'. Meade put the argument that

> public employees, as servants of all the people, have no legal or moral claim to assert a voice in the management of the state's administrative instruments, and the state in turn has no obligation to 'democratize' its administrative organisations, especially where to do so might be seen as subordinating the interests of the masters (the sovereign public) to those of the servants (the public employees). (1971:176)

2 *Alternatively, that representativeness would be appropriate on the grounds of social equity alone.* Referring to industrial democratic processes, Harmon argues that

> the concept of social equity suggests that a public commitment to internal organisational democracy must be unequivocal rather

than contingent upon empirical evidence, demonstrating that organisational democracy (or participative management) leads to greater productivity, efficiency, or even organisational loyalty. (1974:11−12)

3 *That representativeness does not lead to more responsive administrative outcomes*, because of the overwhelming effects of socialisation processes within the bureaucracy. That is, even if, under point 1 above, efficiency is broadly interpreted to include responding better to diverse community demands, the argument is put that the effort will be futile, on the grounds of the 'evidence of rapid value changes of the upwardly mobile' (Subramanium, 1967:1014). I shall return to this point when I discuss the issue of value consensus in the bureaucracy.

4 *That effective administrative reform is not possible until the education system is reformed* (e.g. Hill, 1972). Some argue (e.g. Sheriff, 1974) that the acknowledgment of the role of credentialism in the process of *un*representativeness should not lead to delaying reform; the administrative process needs to be reformed to ensure that it is not *accentuating* the sifting process that occurs within the education system.

5 *That the public sector has a role to play as a 'model employer' and a major employer.* The literature deals with the multiple purposes served by public administration, suggesting that the emphasis on service has obscured its two other significant features: a source of jobs (and therefore economic resources) and a form of citizen participation in a democracy. A stronger form of this argument is based on the premise that the dis-organised and those without resources are in that position as a result of state activity. It is therefore appropriate to put pressure on governments to remedy this situation, by offering employment to those with experiences and perspectives not traditionally sought, as an end in itself and as a means towards more responsive policy formulation.

The approach to the whole question of diversity depends on whether the researcher/practitioner accepts the proposition that administrators — higher and lower — contribute to the policy-formation process, or whether the distinction between the political representative and the impartial administrator is maintained. The argument for representation within the bureaucracy and its relationship to responsiveness to the community is undermined if one accepts this distinction. Yet, even if one does not, it does not necessarily follow that administrative reform is advocated. Again, to quote from Harmon:

the realisation that public administration is inevitably political has long been regarded as one of the major turning points in the

41

history of its academic study ... [But] it made little sense to quarrel about whether administrators should be political actors if nothing could be done about it ... The political realists in public administration stress the importance of understanding the empirical reality of the political world so that what *is* will not be confused with what we would *like to see*. While this reasoning has some face validity, [this view] often implies a convenient rationale for inaction and silence. (1974:13–14)

Before dealing with some of these issues, it is important to discuss what diversity actually means, in relation to affirmative action (AA) initiatives and varying forms of representation. There is a need to comment as well on its supposed association with equity, and its relationship to the merit principle.

DIVERSITY AND AFFIRMATIVE ACTION

We need to distinguish the initiatives around the concept of diversity from the affirmative action initiatives which are already proceeding within the APS and which are directed to women, people of non-English-speaking background, Aboriginal people and people with a disability. The emphasis on diversity is not an affirmative action; it is not a temporary redress measure, but a permanent strategy to widen the social base of the Public Service.

This is not to say that these initiatives are separate in practice, nor that the outcome of one does not affect the outcome of the other. But a strong argument can be put for diversity in the social composition of the APS without there being a strong argument put for affirmative action. That is, merit can be redefined to include experiences and qualities not previously considered, without there being a perceived need to provide special programs for disadvantaged groups. Similarly, people might argue for affirmative action, on the grounds that employment opportunities are not fairly distributed and that positive action is necessary to overcome past and present systemic discrimination. The arguments become linked if it is believed that adequate employment opportunities will be provided through affirmative actions and that the employment of disadvantaged or under-represented groups will ensure more responsiveness to the community.

The main difference between the sets of initiatives is in the idea of representation. Much affirmative action is geared to a redistribution of the workforce, and the success of AA initiatives is partly determined through statistical data on the representation of the targeted groups in different job categories and at different levels in the hierarchy. Diversity, on the other hand, is a concept which refers to a wide range of perspectives and experiences which might be brought into the APS through a redefinition of 'suitability' for jobs; it involves a redefinition of the merit principle, although this redefinition of suitability to incorporate a wider range of skills and experiences is part of the AA program as well.

DIVERSITY AND REPRESENTATION

Diversity as a concept is an expression of the broadening of the merit principle rather than an argument for representation. The emphasis on a diversity of values and experiences is different from traditional notions of representation, in that diversity does not emphasise membership of particular groups. But we need to look at the relationship of diversity to representation, if only because the former is a strategy, in part, to make the bureaucracy more representative of society at large.

The distinction made by Mosher (1968) between active and passive representation is useful, because the concept of diversity comes close to the idea of passive representation — where the bureaucracy 'mirrors' the larger society. But as will be noted when the merit principle is discussed, it is more than that: it aims not only towards representation; it is based on the belief that notions of merit or suitability currently employed are arrived at through a process of exclusion, and constitute a protection of particular, dominant interests.

The idea of passive representation was taken up and further advocated by Kranz in his book *The Pariticipatory Bureaucracy* (1976), where he referred to it as a form of representation which relates to a diversity of perspectives rather than to particular interests.

Active representation, on the other hand, is what we have now, and its extension to include relatively powerless groups is frequently advocated as a means towards more equitable administrative outcomes. It implies a form which is based on individuals representing the interests of a group to which they belong. At the same time that its extension to include underrepresented groups is advocated, writers point to the thorny problems of who represents whom, over what issues, and how is a conflict of interests within groups so represented to be managed? How indeed are groups to be identified as in need of representation? The concept of diversity goes beyond that of active representation in that it seeks not representatives of particular, *identified*, interests, but people with certain characteristics arising out of various experiences which might effectively be brought to bear on a policy issue but which have not been used in the past.

DIVERSITY AND EQUITY

The connection between diversity and administrative outcomes implies the process of achieving more *equitable* outcomes of the administrative process.

The concept of equity is a contested one. Its meaning ranges from equality in treatment and equality in opportunity to equality in outcome. There tends to be an emphasis on the process of distribution of some of society's resources, rather than on the process of production and the allocation of resources around which the social relations of production are organised. As Pateman put it,

> the power structure of the workplace and domestic life are areas of production and reproduction which fall outside the (narrow) distributive concerns of equity ... The individualistic, procedural and ahistorical perspective of equity cannot take account of this dimension of the social structure of liberal democratic societies. (1981:36)

The concept of equity, then, has a problematic relationship to the concept of justice. Yet it may well have more potential as an idea than that of equality (e.g. Kingston, 1981) if leading to an emphasis on outcome, or impact, of social processes on groups with different sets of experiences and with differential access to society's resources.

The concept already appears to be undergoing a practical change in meaning to take account of the bases of inequality which are not captured by the individualistic concept within liberal democratic theory. For example, affirmative actions geared to categories of individuals despite the fortunes of particular individuals within those categories serve to undermine the validity of applying notions of equity only to situations of an individual's access to opportunities. The concept of 'disparate impact' burrows deep into some of the mechanisms and processes by which inequalities of outcome are generated.

My own view is that diversity initiatives will be effective in equity terms only in conjunction with or as an extension of existing EEO programs. The latter are directed towards identified disadvantaged groups which have social movements and pressure groups outside the public service to monitor their effects. Diversity as a strategy does not necessarily rely on these types of links. Indeed, it could well serve to reduce the effectiveness of AA programs. A section of the draft report demonstrates this possibility. It provides examples of how the corporate goals of equity and innovation might be pursued through recruitment: innovation through seeking an entirely new set of recruits from the private sector and equity through the appointment of more people from the identified disadvantage groups. But the appointment of people from disadvantaged categories, in my view, would contribute towards more innovative programs and styles of administration: that is the point of the diversity strategy in general terms. If their appointment were seen simply in 'equity' terms, the potential contribution of such people to innovative policy development and work practices would not necessarily be recognised.

DIVERSITY AND MERIT

Harry Kranz (1974:436) suggests that

> ... the concept of "merit" in public employment has had a rubbery texture, stretching or contracting to cover the prevailing ethos ...

The initiatives dealt with in the draft report explicitly attack the ways in which a narrow definition of merit has been employed in such a way that a variety of experiences, skills, qualities and perspectives have not been introduced into the bureaucracy and have not had a part to play in forming and implementing government policies and programs.

I suggested in my paper that underlying much of the opposition to attempts to broaden the merit principle is the belief that to take into account the experiences, qualifications and perspectives of unrepresented groups is to dilute the merit principle so that other criteria of inclusion, such as that of 'social justice', are being used and are undermining the quality of the service. The assumption here is that the narrow, prevailing definition is the better definition. This is not a proposition developed from examination of alternative possibilities, but a defence of traditional ways of doing things and traditional ways of evaluating people's skills and experiences.

The report effectively asks: who has had the power to define merit in the past? On what grounds can one say that prevailing views of excellence have been inclusive rather than excluding, from the point of view of those subjected to its application? Should we not explore the interests that have adhered to prevailing definitions and applications, and determine whether some people have gained a great deal of power to define what merit means and stand to lose a great deal if it is reassessed from a wider social base?

The report regards the concept of merit as an intrinsically dynamic one. It does this in three quite different ways. First, it argues that the concept of excellence has developed on a fragile base of exclusion. The problem with universalistic criteria of merit is that they 'are intrinsically interconnected with the social structure of privilege and its maintenance' (Duster, 1976:73, cited in Benokraitis and Feagin,

1978:181). Those who have defined it have also sought to insulate it from social transformational processes so that competencies and qualities not traditionally regarded highly remain marginal to the understanding of what is 'meritorious'.

The second way that the report addresses the dynamic nature of the merit, or suitability, principle is by relating it to the particular needs of an area of work at a particular time, thus enabling it to respond to newly uncovered requirements. More emphasis is placed on collective strength than on individual strength, so that suitability for a particular job is geared to the existing capacities of the group. This is not new as we already do this in the determination of selection criteria. What is new is that the qualities being looked for are those not regarded, traditionally, as relevant or valuable.

The third way the dynamic nature of the merit principle is addressed is through the acknowledgment that merit is, in part, a product of organisational processes, of access to opportunities which develop it and which allow for its demonstration. Strategies are suggested which would disperse these opportunities more evenly.

'VALUE-CONSENSUS'

The argument for diversity assumes that value-consensus in the past has been achieved through a selection process which emphasises similarity in outlook, and that socialisation processes in the APS have reinforced this. This situation is defended on the grounds that the prevailing consensus reflects the administrator's impartiality — the consensus is viewed as evidence of value-neutrality.

The issue of value-consensus (or value-'contagion', as Edelman (1974:53) refers to it) relates to the issue of socialisation into a dominant set of values and whether this process offsets the likelihood of a variety of perspectives being brought to bear on policy issues. Most of the discussion on the socialisation effects of the bureaucracy relate to male officers of the working class. Discussion has focused on the somewhat scanty evidence that working-class individuals are more than willing to take on or express the dominant, conservative or middle-class views. The discussion has virtually never referred to the situation of minority groups. But we know that the taking on of white-collar office work by the young men of the working class, whose fathers are in manual labour or the skilled trades, has been a strategic option, viewed as an opportunity for upward mobility in the class structure. The findings, then, are not surprising.

We have to consider the context in which we are discussing diversity. There is an awareness among groups and social movements of the need of the bureaucracy to respond more adequately to their demands. Whether an effective way of doing this is by entry into the bureaucracy is not a cut-and-dried matter. Within the women's movement, for instance, controversy continues over the value of entering as against putting pressure on it from without. But the reality is an influx of women who feel responsible for acting and arguing over policy issues in non-traditional ways. Aboriginal employees appear to be particularly aware of the need to present the views and perspectives of Aboriginal groups. The argument about working-class youths in the past is not one that can be directly applied to these changed circumstances.

The other main difference between the discussions in the literature and what is being attempted in the APS is that the dominant set of values itself is being attacked in the APS. The report acknowledges that to increase representation of a variety of perspectives without a process whereby dominant values are challenged would not be very effective. The report signals an effort to provide a situation in which people will be less likely to be rewarded for adhering to traditional views about appropriate values to hold.

The New Public Administration literature from America certainly acknowledges a need to review the 'mind-set' of the typical administrator. But this is approached in ways that fall short of what is being suggested here. For instance, Harmon speaks of the moral obligation of individuals to be more responsive, and urges the development of mediating structures which would allow for the 'continuous negotiation of meaning' (1981:108). He maintains the distinction between the administrator and the administered, and seems unable to move far from the view of the administrator as needing to be 'benign, competent, socially responsible, . . . imbued with the appropriate democratic values' (Kranz, 1976:42).

But the experience of the unrepresented groups is that to sensitise the administrator to a wider range of values and to set up structures through which they can find expression does not go far enough. For example, as a commentator on the US system said, 'Federal domestic policy is limited now by the overwhelming dominance of people who have directly shared no part of the black experience and who usually neglect' to ask relevant questions about the racial effects of particular policies (Holden, 1973:242−3, cited in Kranz, 1976:94). For many groups, the perspectives represented in the bureaucracy totally exclude their experiences and world-views.

The report rejects the view that the typical administrator can be taught − through staff development, sensitivity training, awareness in dealing with multiculturalism and so on − to become more 're- sponsive': it argues for the importance of direct experience. This is not meant only in relation to the value of it as it is brought into the bureaucracy by particular types of recruits, but the value of Anglo- Australian males learning from working with different people, as

47

colleagues rather than as clients. The 'moral administrator' has a limited capacity to comprehend the sources of alternative social realities, and their validity tends to lie outside his or her scheme of things.

Practical solutions to difficult policy problems are not necessarily brought to the attention of the bureaucracy because of their current 'illegitimacy' and the fear of being penalised. Powerless individuals and groups are frequently quite silent about their particular responses to prevailing attitudes and bureaucratic procedures, and actively develop strategies to avoid their impact. With greater diversity we might find that there are responses to policy issues that have not been available in the past because the knowledge people gain from experience has been marginalised and because not much credence has been given to the value of the ideas of people who have lived with social deprivation in one form or another.

The argument runs that to increase diversity is to provide a rich source of innovative ideas and practical resources for dealing with difficult policy issues, to enlarge the basis on which policy develops, to expand the issues over which negotiation will take place. Negotiation here refers to the processes whereby some agreement is reached on an administrative outcome as a temporary stage in a longer process of contestation and to the continuing process of the 'negotiation of meaning'.

THE IMPLICATIONS FOR CAREERS

The argument for diversity assumes that organisational structures will have to change if different perspectives and the importance of different experiences are to be recognised, protected and, indeed, nurtured. 'The task to be faced is one of *mediation* between diverse arrays of social groups, and hence the task of organising is that of developing mediational organisational structures and strategies'. This would involve, in White's terms, 'a managerial process constantly oriented towards reestablishing equalised power relationships, since these relationships would change through informal dynamics ...' (White, 1971:165, 166).

The draft report implies a reorganisation of typical career paths. Its recommendations challenge the current orthodoxy on the relationship between types of experiences and associated rewards as well as on the processes by which rewarded experience is gained. The ways that work opportunities are distributed will reflect changes in recruitment policy and will tend to encourage the broadening, not the narrowing, of skills and experiences. We are accustomed to defining competence on a narrow, technicist base, whereas the report argues that this may not be the most suitable base from which to operate as a public sector administrator.

Those who have invested in career decisions and in planning ahead are going to resist these changes in recruitment and promotion practices. For example, the literature suggests that on the whole men plan more systematically and over a longer time for their careers than do women. And historically in the APS there has been an association of a career service with Anglo-Australian men. The career-planning process which has been encouraged in the service is lengthy, not only one of accumulating formal educational qualifications but of picking and choosing the work areas in which to gain experience and to cultivate the appropriate relationships with people who might facilitate further progress. All of these activities have been encouraged in the past and the intensity with which they have been carried out is used as an indication of people's motivation to make a contribution to the APS, indeed, as evidence of people's *capacity* to do so. (See Stanton, 1978.)

The objective of diversity throughout the APS is seen in the report as being achieved by questioning any particular degree as an appropriate qualification in positions where it is apparently required. It suggests that there could be an analysis and review of the characteristics, specific task skills, knowledge and perspectives which are thought to be acquired with, or are attributed to, specific formal qualifications to determine whether the same characteristics could be gained from other recruitment sources. Designated groups could be selected to undertake study in fields where there is a particularly high demand in the service.

This means that career paths might become less specialised and more flexible and generalist in nature. Already part of the understanding is that if you enter the Senior Executive Service you must be willing to move around, to transfer from position to position. There is scope here to order quite novel career paths, based on the assumption that the 'understanding' of a variety of perspectives is as important as the accumulation of administrative experience and the practice in one's substantive skill area.

SOME PROBLEMS WITH THE DIVERSITY INITIATIVES

If secondary labour markets are not to develop (or the ghettoisation of minority groups in administrative areas dealing with health and welfare is not to occur) then the examination of the existing credentialism process would have to happen at all levels of the organisation.

This is one of the central problems in the recommendations: that the credentialism process is already an expression of the power of occupational groups to resist changes in the qualifications demanded for particular kinds of work. There is the problem of whether strategies used throughout the Public Service can counter occupational strategies which go beyond the boundaries of public sector employment.

A related problem is that strong traditions are built into the knowledge base and membership of occupational groups, which dictate that some interests are more important than others. What effect, then, would efforts towards diversity and responsiveness have on professional and educational bodies? How effective, for instance, would the public sector be, in reshaping occupational membership and training, the substantive knowledge base and the practice of occupations, through the reorganisation of careers of particular occupational specialists, by demanding a broader knowledge and understanding from those it seeks to recruit? How significant will public sector initiatives be in reshaping management/public administration education? What counter-strategies would develop to undermine the process of developing 'job-related' qualifications?

But the diversity initiatives in conjunction with AA programs have the potential to challenge some of the traditional patterns. Diversity as an initiative on its own has no capacity to reorder in a fundamental way the structuring of opportunities with the APS. Some of the AA initiatives which would need to be developed in association with this initiative include the development of the new career paths discussed above. Without rearrangements in labour markets within the APS a consolidation of the association of certain types of people with low-opportunity jobs would occur.

Although I think movement of people into different types of jobs working with different types of people is a more effective way to change perceptions than training away from the job, nevertheless one AA initiative to reduce this patterning would include a redistribution of training and staff development opportunities. Several years ago I collected samples of advertisements for training opportunities from within a government department. The pattern was clear: for women in low-opportunity jobs, training to consolidate their current skills was offered. For men in high-opportunity jobs, training was directed to advancement and promotion. (See also, Major, 1985, referred to in chapter 2)

The relationship between the diversity initiatives and the development of the SES is also ambiguous, and how it develops in practice depends to a large extent on the effectiveness of the AA program and on the success of some of the strategies referred to above. Major examined the implications of the organisation and training of the SES for training and development officers within the APS (Major, 1984). He discovered the emergence of what could be called a 'new secondary labour market' of trainers who would serve those in 'routine' jobs, while those involved in senior executive development would increasingly be employed as outside consultants or be recruited in laterally. So movement up has been restricted, for a group of people who are in the process of 'professionalising' at the moment, through credentials being offered at tertiary institutions. This process holds its own contradictions. Traditional trainers may not be the ones most suitable for the innovative type of staff development being offered to the SES. Yet the process is occuring of imposing new career ceilings at the same time that AA programs are attempting to dismantle barriers between high- and low-opportunity jobs.

Alternatively, one could examine this situation as an example of how in the past the strategies of particular groups acted as barriers for other groups as far as entry into particular positions was concerned. It might be evidence of a point I have already made, that increasingly it is going to be hard for people to plan well ahead in relation to a narrowly defined career or work area.

Overall, one could conclude by saying that to the extent that the diversity argument highlights processes of power accumulation and the protective and defensive strategies of different groups and occupations, we have a measure of its potential capacity to generate change. However, without the support of a strong EEO program, the main beneficiaries of a diversity stratgy will be women and minorities with professional and technical qualifications. To alter the conditions of employment in such a way that women and minorities in general will have access to advancement opportunities requires the continued development and active implementation of EEO principles in workplace decision-making processes, and a continuing effort to alter the dominant styles and values within the Australian Public Service.

5 The case for a central EEO agency in the Australian Public Service

For the purposes of this chapter, I will assume that the Australian Government *is* interested in and committed to the achievement of equal employment opportunity, not just on the grounds of social justice, but for reasons of productivity and efficiency. But the full use of human resources does not come about at the wave of a wand. It comes about partly through the educative effect of vigorous application of EEO and AA programs. There is another reason for the Government's interest in effective EEO programs: the costs of not having them. These costs are picked up by the Government in the form of providing services to groups and individuals who require them because of exclusion from the labour market.

We need to be clear about what we expect of an effective EEO program. The longer-term outcomes indeed include the integration of EEO principles into all aspects of line managers' functions, so that recruitment, selection, promotion, staff development, training, access to employment opportunities are governed by criteria related to performance and to an individual's capacity to contribute to organisational objectives. But it requires, for a while, the active promotion of such opportunities for members of target groups. Now and in the future, work organisations in Australia will be made up of individuals with a variety of cultural and language backgrounds and with other differences, mainly relating to sex, race, marital status, and extent of able-bodiedness. An integral part of effective management will be a recognition of that diversity in relation to both job performance and the provision of government services. That recognition is still far from being achieved.

In July 1987 the 'letting the managers manage' philosophy for the Australian Public Service emerged with the release of the report by the Efficiency Scrutiny Unit (the Block Report). The establishment of the unit, announced by the Prime Minister to Parliament in September

1986, was part of a broader set of decisions aimed at improving the efficiency of public sector decisions made in the context of the prevailing commitment of the Government for the Australian economy to achieve greater competitiveness in the international marketplace.

The report, in its advocacy of the devolution of administrative and personnel powers and functions to individual agencies (p. 5), recommended the abolition of the Public Service Board and with it the central agency set up to develop and administer EEO policy across the sector. A guiding principle of the unit's work and subsequent recommendations was that

> excessive layers of management and undue volumes of administration are to be eliminated — thus detailed oversight of activities by central agencies is to be avoided — extensive centralised rules and regulations have resulted in many rigidities and inflexibilities in the public sector and the public service in particular — more emphasis is needed on principles and policies and less on rules and regulations. (p. 11)

With the acceptance of the report's recommendations by the Government, we had the beginnings of what has come to be termed the 'mainstreaming' of EEO programs. The word refers to the devolution of the management of the EEO programs to departmental level, the giving to line managers the responsibility for implementing EEO, with corresponding changes in systems of accountability, and the associated dismantling of specialist EEO units.

In such a context, David Block's recommendation of the devolution of responsibility for EEO programs to departmental level can be at best premature, at worst a disaster, not only for members of EEO target groups, but for the Government's own intention to get to the position where full use will be made of human resources within agencies.

Block supports the report's recommendations by reference to similar suggestions made in the 1976 report of the Royal Commission on Australian Government Administration (the Coombs Report) where similar arguments about the efficiency and effectiveness of the proper devolution of authority were made. But we need at least to comment, not only on what else Coombs had to say but on the selectivity of the evidence from both public and private sectors, here and overseas, which Block presents to support his view.

As far as EEO programs were concerned, Coombs insisted that conscious efforts to deal with discrimination in employment were 'still a novel feature of personnel management' (1976:191—92). He believed that an Office of Equality in Employment with a wide-ranging charter should be established to stimulate recruitment, training and career development programs and to monitor their progress (1976:187). He argued that special and urgent action was required in relation to Aboriginal employment, that bold and imaginative programs of special recruitment and training must be set up, with this central office providing assistance to departments in these matters. He recommended the appointment of officers responsible for particular programs, officers with knowledge of and effective communication with the relevant disadvantaged groups (1976:192). This would imply a regional presence.

Block is correct about the trend towards 'divisionalisation', devolution of management decision-making in the private sector. The process, well documented now, supports the view that organisational restructuring is an integral component of corporate strategies, particularly in the case of multinational corporations aiming at maximum flexibility and responsiveness and geared to take advantage of diverse opportunities for further development. But while we can say that the general trend is towards 'leaner organisations, reduced layers of management and decentralised decision-making', we also need to note wide variations in this pattern, and some of the reasons for this.

A book which has won the approval of reviewers and corporate managers alike, not as widely read perhaps as Peters and Waterman's *In Search of Excellence* (1982), but just as soundly based on empirical investigation, is Rosabeth Kanter's *The Change Masters* (1983). Kanter contrasts progressive, highly competitive companies with those which are not doing so well in the marketplace. She has this to say about the human resource management systems which have contributed to higher profitability and financial growth in these companies: they are progressive and innovative. Highly competitive companies rely not just on technical systems and leaner structures but on progressive corporate philosophies. When thoroughgoing organisational change is required, 'centralised power concentration seems to help in the adoption of innovations' (1983:405). She cites the corporate human resource management systems which are set up to provide a coherent framework within which line managers are given responsibility and accountability for personnel decisions (1983:325). She provides many instances of the strong corporate guidance needed to ensure a focus on developing and carrying out innovative programs.

Delegating the personnel function without the prior development of a strong and progressive human resource management system leads to forms of what Kanter calls 'segmentalism' (1983:28). This refers to approaches which deal with problems as narrowly as possible, independently of their context or connections to any other problems. For human resource management it leads to a variety of non-merito-cratic inequities in the treatment of women and minorities (1983:24).

It is not unusual in the private sector to have the delegation of the personnel function to division level and at the same time the retention of some specialist functions at the corporate level.

In the United States there has been some recentralising of the EEO function in the private sector, as with other functions where statutory requirements are strict and non-compliance may be expensive. We cannot predict what the patterns are going to be in the private sector in Australia. Neither Block nor I can speculate on the extent to which, in their response to the affirmative action legislation, companies will decide on strong central guidance and control of EEO programs. To the extent that EEO is seen as a means to capitalise on human resources to give organisations a competitive edge, we will find a strong EEO presence at corporate level.

We can question, too, whether such a decentralised structure is, in all respects, an appropriate one for a constellation of public sector agencies. In New York State, for example (the tenth largest employer in the U.S.), there is a commitment to a strategic approach to the systematic management of human resources. Walter Broadnax, while President of the NY State Civil Service Commission, in October 1987 addressed a State Civil Service Management Conference and outlined the 'state view'. He used the analogy of a wagon wheel and its spokes: the state positions itself to deal with demographic and market changes, with a state-wide human resources management strategy, which is developed collaboratively and reflexively, to allow for 'mid-course corrections as we move into the next century' (Broadnax, 1987).

Block's reference to overseas public services, in Canada, the United States and New Zealand, is too brief to allow for any real assessment of the extent to which various functions have been devolved. For example, in Canada, the Civil Service Commission was abolished in 1967, as Block points out. But one of the agencies which took on some of its functions—the Treasury Board Secretariat—has several advisory committees dealing with the employment of different groups. The government sets targets which departments are expected to meet and there is tight monitoring and audit control of EEO programs.

Block refers to State governments as well as to overseas public services to support his restructuring proposals. It is a pity that he did not separate out the EEO function from the more general personnel function when he looked for his examples. There are significant instances of the strengthening of the EEO function at central level. In Victoria, for example, the units dealing with both Aboriginal and women's employment have been strengthened recently. In the Northern Territory, the recruitment program for Aboriginal employees has been recentralised, because there was virtually no progress while it was left to individual departments. In South Australia base-grade clerical recruitment remains centralised and the Department of Personnel and Industrial Relations is responsible for the recruitment of Aboriginal people and people with disabilities. In New South Wales there is a central agency dealing with EEO in the public sector alongside a strong philosophy of 'letting the managers manage'.

To sum up, there are many variations within the general shift towards devolution of management responsibilites. As John Child, among others, consistently reminds us (for example, 1984:242), there is no one 'best way' to structure organisations. Much of the variation is a matter of 'strategic choice' and much of it depends upon corporate philosophy.

ARE DEPARTMENTS READY FOR EEO RESPONSIBILITIES?

The most persuasive argument for doing away with a central agency concerned with EEO programs in the public services would be evidence that EEO is already a part of the normal everyday practice of line managers within departments. Such evidence would include at least the following.

- The head of the agency is publicly identified with a strong commitment to integrating EEO principles into all management decision-making processes.

- The EEO program is closely linked at all relevant points in the overall corporate planning process.

- Line managers are accountable for relevant EEO progress and their achievements are assessed in the review of their performance.

- Reviews of human resources management policies and practices have táke account of knowledge of the ways in which bias against members of EEO groups enter these processes. Implementation of these systems is monitored to ensure the systems remain clear of such bias.

- Changes in job design, career structures and job integration strategies are based on informed assessments of the nature and value of work currently being performed.

- Alongside the provision of special programs for target group members, an emphasis has been placed on assessing organisational values, traditions, customs and practices which create artificial barriers to the advancement of EEO groups.

- All organisational change is informed by EEO principles.

- The organisation actively investigates new or different ways that jobs might be performed effectively and this is reflected in selection criteria.

- There is continuing consultation with staff associations and members of the EEO groups.

- Training and development programs are, among other things, geared to have a redistributive effect on the workforce, and mechanisms exist to monitor this effect.

- Recruitment programs for Aboriginal people and people with a physical disability are bold and imaginative, and key appointments reflect the priority given in these areas.

- Corporate philosophy and employment practices reflect the reality of a diverse and multicultural society.

- Corporate responsibility is retained for policy development and the monitoring of progress with regard to the more sensitive and intractable EEO issues.

- A comprehensive personnel data base exists to facilitate strategy development and workforce planning.

- Compliance with EEO legislative requirements is routinely examined during management audits conducted within agencies.

- The corporate planning process has the capacity to address issues of indirect and structural discrimination.

- Steady progress over a period of years has been made in reducing concentrations of target groups' members in particular classifications, and in reducing the sex segmentation of the workforce.

- The nature and delivery of public services equate with the needs and circumstances of the varied client groups.

If the EEO function is devolved to departmental level at the present time this will mean the end of what effective programs there are. There is no evidence that the EEO function has been incorporated into broader corporate objectives at the departmental level. The reality is that few officers understand what is involved and even fewer attempt to put their understanding into practice.

Until recently little empirical work had been carried out in Australia to inform organisational strategies. For example, there was no

Australian research into sex and race bias in job evaluation, classi-fication systems, performance appraisal, supervisor perceptions of training and development needs or job allocation practices. Some of this empirical work has been done (see Burton et al., 1987; and see other chapters in this book) and shows how subtle and pervasive such biases are, and how apparently minor decisions accumulate to affect the distribution of different sorts of people among job cat-egories within organisations. In America this type of data has had a significant impact on several personnel practices, because of the more stringent compliance requirements that exist there (for example, Lansbury, 1981:xvi; McLane, 1980:150).

The evidence on the complexity of the processes and the multiplicity of ways in which people can be disadvantaged in the workplace needs to be collected, assimilated and translated into policy advice and guidelines. It would be impossible for this level of activity to be carried out by individual departments. It can only be done by a central personnel agency. The target groups — and this is why they are identified under the legislation — are the relatively powerless in organisations. Strong central support is needed for the programs directed to them.

COSTS OF DEVOLVING THE EEO FUNCTION

What are some of the costs of devolving the EEO function to de-partmental level?

It would be a waste of resources for principles to be formulated for recruitment, selection and promotion by a Public Service Commission without guidelines, information and research relevant to implement-ation. In reality government departments manifest a narrow concern with their own functions, and lack a wider, innovative, experimental style and view. Potentially vital principles which departments do not see as part of their short-term interest would not be translated into practice.

This would constitute a premature integration of the EEO function into line management before the function is either understood or accepted.

There would be internal costs. At present the two main justi-fications for the low classification level of EEO coordinators are that there is a central resource unit providing policy guidelines on which the coordinator can rely and that the coordinator reports to a senior officer, who is responsible for the EEO program in the department. The reality is that senior staff responsible for EEO programs are busy executives who leave the day-to-day work to the coordinator. Without a central agency providing policy advice and monitoring progress, the EEO coordinator, to be effective, would have to take on some of the central agency functions and the position would need to be significantly upgraded. The more likely outcome, given the abolition of the statutory requirement to report to a central EEO agency, is the withdrawal of resources from EEO at department level.

Without central guidance, EEO would not develop in a consistent manner within the public service, and variations in practice would be significant. This would result in a lack of overall policy within the APS. The Public Service then runs the risk of losing control of general policy directions.

There would probably be an increase in complaints from staff within departments to anti-discrimination agencies, in the form of individual and class actions. People's expectations are high and disadvantaged individuals will pursue their employment rights in one arena if the possibilities for redress are blocked in another.

Many of the people running organisations as policy-makers and policy-implementers, as personnel officers or executive team members, have insufficient commitment to EEO principles and do not really believe they are necessary. Such managers do not have the knowledge to be confident that EEO programs will result in a beneficial cleaning up of personnel policies and practices and are anxious lest they result in disruption and conflict. There is little appreciation of the fact that the merit principle has been applied in conservative and rigid ways, thereby promoting sameness and a degree of mediocrity. There is widespread belief that equity for women, Aboriginal people, people from non-English-speaking backgrounds and people with physical or intellectual disabilities means treating them as if they are the same as able-bodied white males. The prevailing norms, values and understandings with which white males are comfortable are deemed the most appropriate for all people. Managers frequently believe that the traditional ways of doing things are the most efficient simply because they know of no other ways to perform or organise the work.

THE BENEFITS OF A CENTRAL EEO AGENCY

A central agency with statutory power to review EEO programs and implementation provides incentive for departments and authorities to put resources into the area. Moreover, such a central agency gives EEO officers at relatively low classification levels resources to bargain with, to support their recommendations, to clarify their own goals, to persuade others and to develop their change strategies. It provides training and staff development resources across departments, avoiding replication costs. It brings together the knowledge learnt from successful and unsuccessful strategies across departments. It extracts what is common to organisations and distinguishes this from the particular contexts that individual organisations might confront. It provides personnel officers with important resources in the form of selection and other guidelines.

Through comparative analysis, a central agency provides annual reports on the critical as distinct from the marginal effects of particular strategies and on the effective use of particular resources. It disseminates research findings and distils them for most effective use at departmental level. It maintains close contacts with other corporate developments, thus facilitating the integration of EEO with other objectives. It facilitates the shift of the function to the corporate arena and down through line managers. It assesses future directions for the service as a whole.

The central agency monitors progress, reducing and refining the type of data needed to measure effectiveness (O'Farrell and Harlan, 1984:286). It provides technical assistance to improve the process of establishing goals (numerical and structural), timetables, and performance standards. It is in a position to distinguish changes in employment patterns which derive from alterations in labour market conditions, from changes which are the outcomes of direct interventionist EEO strategies. In this way data from across the Public Service, and indeed from the labour market generally, rather than merely from individual departments, can be used to evaluate the effectiveness of EEO programs.

Commonwealth policy must strengthen the incentives for change at the level of individual departments (O'Farrell and Harlan, 1984:286) and facilitate that change through the availability of training and other programs and resources. This can best be done by retaining the central agency with statutory responsibility for reviewing EEO performance, as well as the support functions outlined above.

EEO represents a particular, and substantial, intervention in the labour market. Like other such interventions such as industry-restructuring strategies, this intervention will necessarily involve complex performance indicators. These will require careful research, continuing development and close and perceptive monitoring.

Either EEO is done properly, or it should be abandoned. Otherwise we are wasting valuable resources, time and energy. Moreover, through the promise of EEO, we are raising people's expectations only to dash those expectations through lack of program support, with all the predictable social repercussions. Members of the target groups have a right to know: is EEO a serious government policy or is it a gesture, a symbolic statement without substance? If it is to be taken seriously, let us recognise the field of expertise for what it is: a body of complex knowledge, still in the early stages of development, but sophisticated enough to be able to provide significant support for the introduction of more efficient and less discriminatory work practices within public secter agencies.

6 Job redesign and the Australian Public Service

In many countries — America, Great Britain, Scandinavia — work reorganisation schemes are occurring, for the same sorts of reasons that they are emerging here: from the need to promote more efficient work practices, to increase productivity, to cut costs. And in each country, too, the demands from the workforce, through their unions, mean that the only practical way of reorganising is to move from Tayloristic methods of increased specialisation and deskilling to multiskilling, which includes the removal of demarcations, the use of generic job titles reflecting job enlargement, and broadbanding, (bringing together within a single grade or classification jobs previously separately graded or classified).

The benefits to management, through flexibility in the use of employees' skills and experiences, are clear. But how do we ensure that the overall effect of work reorganisation will enhance the employment opportunities available to women and members of other disadvantaged groups who have, by and large, been restricted to low-status, low-paying, low-opportunity jobs?

The outcomes of work reorganisation are open-ended (Rose and Jones, 1985:83); the shape and direction it takes depend very much on one's involvement. One can write a blueprint for the future, one can draw connections between reorganisation, job redesign and job satisfaction, and productivity. But there is nothing inevitable about these connections. Certain structural arrangements make some things more possible, and other things less possible, but they don't guarantee anything. Nothing just happens. Everything depends upon what people *do*, day by day, at the workplace, and the power they have to influence the outcomes. The booklet produced by the Joint Council Sub-Committee on Industrial Democracy lists these principles of work reorganisation and good job design, and indicates the importance of participative processes (Office of the Public Service Board, 1987). It emphasises the requirement to train staff, including specialist

61

staff, union delegates and officials, supervisors and managers. It does not, though, emphasise enough the need to ensure that present inequalities in access to advancement opportunities are not carried into the new office structure. The booklet shares this problem with most of the work design literature, which has had little to say about, for example, the gender structuring of organisations.

What does it mean to say that we have to take into account, in the redesign process, the gender structuring of organisations? At the broadest level, we can say that men and women are to be found in different jobs, different occupations, and, where mixed, different hierarchical levels within classifications and occupations, with women at the lower ends. It has been said that gender is one key element of 'customary law' at the workplace, that gender is a powerful basis for clustering jobs in promotion ladders, and for the position of jobs within those ladders (Baron et al., 1986:251, 270).

Much decision-making in organisations is based on perceptions of what is appropriate work, or training, or development, or courses of study, or task allocation for people because of their sex, race or other social characteristic. The allocation of jobs on the basis of *gender* appears to be so ingrained in organisations that these practices seem to be 'natural', and therefore part of the fixed, and unchangeable, structure of organisations (Rosenbaum, 1984:209). They have not, then, been a target for change as far as work reorganisation practitioners are concerned.

Attention to gender is justified when one considers that women constitute the bulk of job occupants at the lower levels of the APS. In the newly created structure, it has been estimated that women will make up 72 per cent of Level 1 positions and 64 per cent of Level 2 positions, dropping to 44 per cent at Level 3. People from keyboard and clerical assistant classifications will account for 82 per cent of Level 1 officers (Winters, pers. comm.). Of course, when you look at these categories, you find that race and ethnicity are also important factors.

It has always been my view that EEO principles should be informing all organisational activity and organisational change processes. Rarely, if ever, has this occurred. I have argued since EEO came to the public sector (e.g. Burton, 1985) that job redesign should be a central component of all EEO programs. Since this has never been the case, I am arguing here that EEO needs to be a central component of all job redesign efforts. If jobs have, among other things, a gender base, and yet we aim, through our EEO programs, to redistribute men and women across jobs and occupations, then clearly without job redesign we have an uphill battle.

The gender base of job design contributes to the exclusion of men from women's jobs and vice versa. This would be bad enough if what women and what men are supposed to do were deemed equally important, but it is much worse when what is seen as appropriate for women is consistently of a lower status and of less importance than what men do, because women lose out on important opportunities for developing skill and knowledge, not to mention influence and higher incomes.

When we talk about integrating typing and keyboard and secretarial positions with clerical and administrative work, we are talking about dismantling a system of job structures which was based on assumptions about women's lack of rights to, and interest in, careers.

In the Australian Public Service, the central EEO agency's role in advising on and monitoring EEO progress is now a smaller one, so it is more crucial that EEO principles be built into organisational structures, so that there is less capacity for individuals with outmoded assumptions about women's work commitments to contribute to women's disadvantaged status. In other words, building EEO principles into the work reorganisation and job redesign process is a significant long-term strategy to achieve equality in access to employment opportunities.

But formal rules and organisation design do not, by themselves, lead to such equality. So, although principles of redesign are very important, so is the retraining of managers and supervisors into an awareness of how their daily practices can disadvantage members of the target groups. Without the monitoring of managers' achievements in the development of their subordinates, efforts made in job redesign will have a smaller effect than is desired on skill development, morale, turnover, and job satisfaction.

Good redesign principles are contained in the Joint Council booklet (see also Hackman and Oldham, 1980). The following pages set out the fifteen principles that are important if we are to eliminate the gender, race and other bases to job design and job allocation. The intention of such processes is to ensure that women and members of other disadvantaged groups have equitable access to jobs or tasks that provide for the demonstration of 'merit', that provide for skill development and that have advancement opportunities built into them. The other side of this coin is that we have to be sure that jobs are not designed to be more suitable for one sex or the other when this is not necessary for effective job performance.

All the principles of good redesign apply to jobs regardless of whether the current or potential occupants are male or female, people with or without physical disabilities, are of English or non-English-speaking background, are Aboriginal or non-Aboriginal, and so on. The flexibility within each work level should allow retention of the principles, while accommodations can be made from time to time in response to the needs and requirements of individuals such as those with disabilities.

1 The first job redesign principle is to eliminate aspects of jobs which reduce advancement opportunities, and build in aspects which enhance them.

'Vertical loading' is a phrase that refers to building into jobs at lower levels aspects of higher-level jobs so that the occupant is prepared for advancement. 'Diagonal loading' (Janson, 1975:304) refers to this in a more extensive way, and means pulling down to lower levels aspects of a range of jobs from a higher level, opening up a wider range of possible movements upwards from a particular job. This sort of flexibility in job movement seems to be intended by the designers of the new structure. Its broad work-level descriptions reflect these processes, in that these principles of vertical and diagonal loading have informed the decision to broadband and to operate, within each level, with generic duty statements.

In the design of particular jobs and in the training opportunities afforded to job occupants, it is important to retain this flexibility, so that potential movements from one job to another are not unduly restricted. To illustrate: if word processing is seen as a natural basis on which to train job occupants in more complex data-processing and programming work, rather than as a basis for moving into clerical/administrative work, the occupant of positions with a relatively larger component of word processing will be unnecessarily restricted in options for movement.

2 No job should be designed on the assumption that typical occupants are female, and neither should they be designed on the basis that the typical occupant lacks career interest, is unintelligent, or has a preference for routine work.

Levels 1 and 2 positions in the Public Service must be looked at particularly carefully with this principle in mind. The descriptions of work levels higher than 1 and 2 tell us a great deal about good job design with Levels 1 and 2. What is expected at higher levels tells us about feeder and bridging tasks and functions, and the experiences and skills that need to be developed. For example, the Level 2 description includes some supervisory work, and knowledge of Acts and Regulations, which indicate the possible content of training programs provided at the level below.

3 *All* jobs should have feeder/bridging tasks and functions. While or where this is not possible, job rotation practices should be guided by the requirement for all workers to have access to jobs with such tasks and functions.

Job rotation as usually practised performs different functions for different categories of workers. Simply put, at lower levels it has been used to relieve boredom and routine, and to create some flexibility for managers, but has tended to be restricted to rotating people from one routine job to another. The purpose of job rotation at higher levels (in the Senior Executive Service, for example) is to enhance career prospects, to develop a person's organisational knowledge, contacts with other people, familiarity with the work of other units and areas, to socialise people into the prevailing ethos and culture of the Public Service and of particular agencies.

In this and in other ways, we can often learn, selectively, from practices higher up in the organisation what might be possible further down. Job rotation contributes to EEO if it is designed to enhance experience, skills and knowledge, to make people more able to move to new positions which have further opportunities attached. It also contributes to EEO in its capacity to undermine strong, traditional subcultures at the workplace, the sort that tend not to be welcoming to outsiders, people of a different sex, colour, or cultural background (Kanter, 1977:283).

This is where job redesign and work reorganisation affect each other. Within the clerical assistant and clerical administration streams, as they previously existed, some areas of work were known by agency personnel as more 'dead-end' than others. So when a vacancy occurred, some people would be encouraged into it and others discouraged, depending on the value that work experience in the area might have. There is a great deal of evidence to show that women are more likely to be streamed into the dead-end areas than men. This is an *organisational* practice, one of job allocation, not a practice which reflects women's preferences or choices.

Research into one Commonwealth department (PJ 1987) pointed to the allocation of male and female clerical assistants to 'cells', as they are called, solely on the basis of the opportunity structures that existed in them. Females were placed in those cells where there were few levels of clerical assistant positions and no history of mobility into clerical grades, and the men into cells where there were more levels and a history of movement out of clerical assistant into clerical grades. The recruits do not know this, and by the time they are in their work areas they are already affected by allocation. There is a labelling process going on whereby some people in some dead-end areas are thought of as dead-end people, and they have little opportunity, in their routine jobs, to demonstrate otherwise.

In instances of recruitment into clerical grades, too, one is likely to find that women are allocated to areas where the jobs are more routine, where less on-the-job training occurs, often in the belief that the women will leave to have children, and the training would be wasted on them. After several years of tracing a cohort one is likely to find that the women are in fewer work areas, even when they predominate numerically, and are not as widely distributed among hierarchical levels as men.

This discrimination in initial job assignment achieves its significance through the ways it feeds into other forms of discrimination later on. In more than one empirical investigation it has been found that jobs and assessments in an employee's early years 'have profound and enduring effects on later career outcomes' (Rosenbaum, 1979:223; see also Rosenbaum, 1984; Newman, 1982; Veiga, 1983). But men and women are not evenly distributed among jobs which allow for a demonstration of capacity to advance.

We know that ability and 'potential' are notoriously difficult to define, identify and measure. So we tend to use indicators of them, and education, training and years of experience have played a significant role here. But something else does, too. People's job history appears to be used as a significant indicator of ability and potential (Rosenbaum, 1984:273, 279). This means, in particular, that the paths taken through an organisation and the time taken to get to a particular position are important for assessments of one's capacity for further advancement.

But the job assignment practices of organisations mean that two people, equally qualified and competent, as a result of assignment to a challenging and routine job, will have quite different opportunities to demonstrate and develop their capacities. I am not referring to individual differences here, but to the systematic allocation of women and members of other disadvantaged groups to the more routine of jobs on offer.

4 Since job history acts as a proxy for ability, all other things being equal, we have a responsibility to ensure that job allocations are made without regard to personal attributes which are irrelevant to job performance. I have already indicated that challenging tasks need to be evenly distributed among jobs within each work level.

5 Until 'dead-end' areas can be transformed, by applying new technologies in ways consistent with the reorganisation efforts being embarked on, people should be recruited to them without regard to gender. They should, once recruited there, be rotated out of them before they are contaminated by the dead-endedness of such work areas, in their own minds or in the perception of others (see Winters, 1987:12).

Many women believe they have the ability to progress and feel 'caught' in their jobs, and many feel that supervisors do not appreciate their job demands (e.g. as expressed by workers in the review of keyboard structures (Public Service Board, 1984)). Whether as the result of fear of reprisal or pressures to act in certain ways, or believing that nothing would be achieved by trying, many women will not act on their own behalf, either as individuals or through their unions.

There are pressures on women to display stereotypical behaviour and aspirations, and these pressures might well be stronger from supervisors and middle managers than from top managers (Izraeli and Izraeli, 1985), which would imply a barrier to be got through, after which competent women will find organisational life somewhat easier. To the extent that these pressures exist, women are held back from expressing interest in certain types of jobs or tasks. This allows supervisors to overlook the potential contributions of women to a wide range of positions.

This is a particularly important issue for women with keyboard, typing and secretarial backgrounds. There is evidence of a stigma attached to this work, and evidence that a history in this kind of job is not highly valued in organisations. People in these positions tend not to receive positive assessments of their capacity to advance.

Some of the occupants of these positions are likely to resist change, for a couple of reasons. One is that they will feel they are losing something — work that they received satisfaction from and which used their particular skills. In the 1984 keyboard review, it was found that many operators regarded the routine clerical work around them as less skilled than their own. This means that meaningful, satisfying, challenging work must be built into the jobs which these people take up.

They will also resist change because they will be uncertain that they can handle what is going to be expected of them. We have to acknowledge, here, the accumulated effect that work in those positions has on occupants. Kanter (1977:98) describes the secretaries in her study as being made, through good performance at their jobs, less and less fit for other jobs. The documentation she provides of attempts to integrate secretarial workers into clerical structures should sensitise us to some of the problems ahead and the requirements for support, adequate training (of occupants and their managers) and thoughtful job rotation.

Not all occupants of these positions, of course, will be anxious or resisting. For some, this will be an opportunity long awaited. For others, the extra effort put into training, and good, constructive feedback on progress and job performance will be all that is required for a positive attitude towards taking up new opportunities.

Of course, the training of more experienced keyboard operators and secretaries, those who have been in the service in those positions for a longer time, will be different from that provided for those who have recently entered or who enter now, to take account of the effects, to which I have referred, of being in the job for a consider-able period.

Care must be taken, though, not to assume that people need to attain skills that they in fact already have. This can easily happen because, for example, secretaries are not *seen* to be running offices, to be engaged in clerical and administrative work, though in fact they are doing so. Similarly, the labels 'supervisor' and 'manager' have been placed on positions in the past depending, to a large degree, on whether the people supervised are in male-dominated or female-dominated jobs. It may that there are women with managerial skills who have not been acknowledged as having them.

Thus there are dangers in assuming that it is female job occupants who need all the training. It might be that their supervisors and managers need training in identifying and drawing upon skills and experiences that have gone unacknowledged. On the other hand, specific training to do work in redesigned jobs *is* needed and senior Public Service staff will have to ensure that it is given, even though the pressure might be there from clerical workers to receive keyboard skills as a priority. Because keyboard workers do not clamour for it as loudly does not mean it is less important.

Managers and job occupants alike have anxieties about whether a person can 'cope' with new job challenges. This is partly justified, since many jobs have traditionally been designed to be so routine and boring they produce what has been called 'trained *in*capacity' (Kanter, 1977:98). However, the evidence from the literature is clear that renewed enthusiasm, interest and capacity result from new job challenges, supported, of course, by adequate retraining.

We have to be aware, when constructing multiskilled and flexible jobs within a work level, that different processes of work *allocation* might occur in apparently identical jobs and have quite different effects on people's opportunities to advance in the organisation. I have observed, in public sector agencies, the very different treatment and encouragement given by supervisors to lower-graded male and female clerical staff. Perceptions are important here, rather than a conscious intent to discriminate. The discretionary power of super-visors is likely to be exercised in such a way that when odd tasks crop up that are interesting or different, a young male will be allocated to them. But in addition, it appears that the idea of a male as a breadwinner operates in people's minds and affects their perceptions of people's needs and aspirations. So when opportunities are scarce, a young male is more likely to be perceived as disadvantaged by a lack of career opportunities and thus will be encouraged to take opportunities up when they arise.

As well, when people are being assessed for their promotability, 'social behaviours' appear to be more important in the assessment of people from minority groups than for members of the majority group (e.g. Cox and Nkomo, 1986). Whether a person 'fits in' to the organisational culture and traditional ways of doing things assumes importance in the assessment of minority staff, at the expense of potentially new and innovative ways of effectively performing in jobs.

6   All jobs should provide opportunities for skills (or 'merit') to be demonstrated, to be noticeable. Some important aspects of this are physical mobility and contact with a wide range of other jobs and people; visibility (the 'backbone' of the office usually works in the back room and is often a position where the occupant and her skills go unrecognised) and boundary-spanning, where the occupant is in contact with other units and/or other organisations and is more likely to get feedback on performance from a variety of people, including clients (see Kanter, 1977:177, 179, 253; Hackman and Oldham, 1980:104).

7   Public contact work, or the allocation of tasks that bring people into contact with other organisations and people in other work areas, needs to be carefully distributed among jobs. Some public contact work is routine and some is not. Some of this work has traditionally been viewed as requiring a worker of one sex or another.

I have noticed that supervisors tend to allocate work that involves contact with other organisations more often to males than to females. Sometimes the reason given is that transport across the city is awkward, but often it is that the client organisation would not be responsive to a female representative or that a response will be slower if a female asks for a report or for a task to be performed. This argument is also used to bar people from a non-English-speaking background, people of a different colour, and people with disabilities, from public contact positions. I have already noted the importance of the availability of this type of work to the full range of employees.

The process of allocating people to jobs in a way that will not offend customers or clients has been called consumer-based discrimination, and it is widespread. To allocate work on the basis of sex or colour or personal appearance is to perpetuate the community's images of appropriate job-holders. These apparently trivial differences in work allocations are huge in their impact on different workers' experiences on the job.

It is important to emphasise the value of staff dealing with others, receiving feedback from them, and, through their job demands, needing to acquire further knowledge of the links the agency has with outside bodies. It generates formal and informal contacts, increases the information the occupant has about the workings of different areas, and, it appears, contributes to confidence and self-esteem.

8   What has to be looked at carefully are the 'personal' support services components of jobs (see Roos and Reskin, 1984:251). Work in some jobs which provide support services to other jobs are good learning experiences and training grounds for advancement; others are not. Typing, word processing and stenographic support services have not, traditionally, been highly rewarded at the workplace and have not been seen as work experiences that can be built upon in clerical and administrative work.

While I know that one of the intentions of the restructuring is to open up career opportunities for women who have these skills, there are some problems raised by the way this work has been organised in the past. Typing, word processing and, to a lesser extent, stenographic skills have traditionally been associated with low career ceilings. Effective job redesign means breaking that association, so that those skills can be used with higher-level clerical/administrative skills. But on the other hand the skills are, almost by definition, used to support the work of a higher-level officer.

This issue has to be tackled early on. The paradox, commented on regularly in the literature, is that women, with their *extra* keyboard skills, have been penalised, partly through a stigma that is attached to such work and thus the people performing it. It is seen as routine and mechanical and not involving much skill. The research in my book *Women's Worth* (1987) demonstrates the ignorance which people have about the capacities and skills drawn on by the occupants of many keyboard positions. Accurate and fast keyboard work is required as a support service to many job occupants, but it is virtually always at the expense of the career or advancement opportunities of the people performing it.

9   The language used to describe work levels and individual jobs must be free of sex-linked terms. An example of this is provided in the work-level descriptions, where 'receptionist duties' under Level 1 are mentioned. But what these duties *are*, the knowledge and inter-personal skills their performance requires, is not spelled out. This is public contact work and needs to be described properly for the experience and the skill requirements to become clear. To refer to duties as 'receptionist' duties conjures up an image of a woman. To refer to them in terms which describe the actual work involved allows for a wider range of potential occupants, men or women.

The use of vague words to describe some work obscures the complexity of it, or the particular features of it, and this feeds into the impression given of the attributes the person doing the job has, or is accumulating. The phrase 'ability to *work on* a wide range of office equipment' denies the knowledge and skill base developed through training and experience in operating the equipment. Words which need to be used with care are 'routine', 'straightforward', 'personal' (providing personal support to another officer usually requires certain knowledge and skills which need to be stated, and attention needs to be drawn to the fact that it is *organisational* work being performed), and 'familiarity' ('familiarity with the functions of related work areas' implies knowledge of certain matters, and an ability to *do* something through experience).

I make this point because the choice of words, we discovered in the research I referred to earlier, has a lot to do with the sex of the typical occupant of jobs. In public contact work, for example, men's jobs sounded more important than women's, because they were described as 'presenting a good public image of the organisation, liaising with outside bodies', and women's as being 'courteous' and having a 'pleasant telephone manner'. In other words, we felt that sex-linked phrases were used to describe aspects of jobs which required similar activity, but the description of the women's work made it sound less difficult than it really was. The relative assessment of the experiences and capacities of the occupants of these jobs would be different, should they apply for other positions.

As I said earlier, one can redesign something on paper, but it is people's behaviour and their practices at the workplace that make it effective or not. If one decides to multi-skill jobs and enlarge the experience and skills that people accumulate at the workplace, one has to do more than redesign jobs and reorganise work. The arrangements and practices surrounding the redesigned jobs need to be consistent with and supportive of the desired outcomes of the work reorganisation process. To be consistent, too, with EEO principles, such practices would involve the active promotion of the opportunities of people whose previous jobs limited their advancement prospects.

10   Clearly there is a need to train and educate managers and supervisors in the changed requirements of their roles, now that those they are supervising have greater flexibility and responsibility in the work they are performing. The literature is replete with examples of the obstacles which supervisors present to participatory work reorganisation programs. The lack of supervisory and management commitment to the changes, many authors claim (e.g. Bailey, 1983), is probably the single most common cause of failure of work-restructuring efforts. One book on the subject is more specific, suggesting that it is middle managers, more than supervisors or top managers, who are best positioned to make the work reorganisation succeed or fail. The authors say:

We have often observed middle managers assume a distant, 'wait and see' stance toward work redesign activities undertaken by their subordinate managers or by organizational consultants. In our view, such a stance is ill-advised. For it is the behavior of middle managers, perhaps more than any other single factor, that ultimately determines whether work redesign turns out to be a success or yet another 'good idea that doesn't work in the real world'. (Hackman and Oldham, 1980:157)

Another writer points out: 'Structure and style are interrelated. Work structuring and the development of organization designs that permit greater autonomy at the level of the job imply the need for a delegated style of management' (Bailey, 1983:191).

Not only is extensive training required to shift supervisors from a directing and controlling mode to a developmental one (Bailey, 1983:210; see also Lansbury and Gilmour, 1986), but their job descriptions and duty statements must also reflect their changed responsibilities. The work-level descriptions will probably need revising to deal with issues of this kind.

11   The evaluation of managers' performance must account for their changed role and the increased responsibility for the development, through job assignment and other practices, of all their subordinates. Here too, the literature is clear on the possible obstacles to progress on this front: 'The majority of managers will underemphasise their role in developing subordinates in favour of duties that are measured and rewarded, unless this responsibility is built into their duties and is evaluated and rewarded through the same processes as other aspects of performance that are evaluated' (McEnery and Lifter, 1987:75).

To the extent that supervisors and managers are involved in selecting staff, determining the allocation of specific assignments and evaluating employees' performance, in promotion decisions, advising or determining who will be selected for what training and development opportunities (Fear and Ross, 1983:24), providing encouragement and support in career planning, they have a central responsibility for the equitable outcomes of the reorganisation and should themselves be assessed on their effectiveness in implementing it.

12   It is necessary to educate managers and supervisors to be equitable in their treatment of men and women and members of disadvantaged groups. When we discuss effective and equitable work reorganisation and job redesign we are not just talking about the EEO principles that inform the process. Good redesign principles *are* EEO principles. Even if the APS were not dealing with attempts to promote the advancement of the target groups, the principles would remain. Because members of the disadvantaged groups are clustered

in low-opportunity jobs, however, we have a strong obligation to ensure that the office restructuring *contributes to*, rather than inhibits, their access to interesting and challenging work.

The importance of ensuring non-discriminatory and equitable daily practices of supervisors and middle managers cannot be overemphasised when one considers their role in determining people's suitability for particular opportunities or work experiences. They are strategically placed to determine the fate of many of the people working under them. There is a need for insights into the ways in which the new organisational arrangements could create new, or reinforce existing, inequalities, unless mechanisms are built in to avoid it happening.

We are concerned to ensure that management practice does not result in the streaming of different types of people into different kinds of jobs, detrimentally affecting some people's opportunities to advance and also productivity levels (discrimination is, after all, a most inefficient work practice). We want to minimise the possibility of newly created men's jobs and women's jobs emerging, and a 're-ghettoisation' of women and members of other disadvantaged groups (see O'Farrell and Harlan, 1984:276). Attention to this issue means more emphasis than the work reorganisation literature is inclined to give to structures of opportunity and power. Kanter points this out when she says:

> The things that need to be taken into account in job enrichment (and more broadly, in systematic work redesign) are not confined to aspects of the work itself and its immediate supervisory context; they require attention to structures of opportunity and power ... 'job satisfaction' measures tied to job attributes may miss the most critical element shaping people's relationships to their work and commitment to the organization: the opportunity structure ...
>
> There are many indications that job enrichment and work redesign stand or fall in practice by their effects — or lack of them — on opportunity and power structures. (1977:256)

13 The type and cost of training that is provided, and to whom, need to be monitored. I am sometimes told that women receive their share of training in the APS, but I'm not so sure. If one took into account the type of training that is provided (See chapter 2) it would appear that women are less likely, for example, to be selected for supervisory training than men (Ruble et al., 1984:348). In the United States,

> Aggregate data compiled by the U.S. Civil Service Commission (1977) show that white males are more likely to receive training than any other minority/sex group; that when they do receive training, white males receive more hours of training; and that

their average cost of training is greater than that received by any other minority/sex group. (Taylor, 1985:69)

It was also found that, after controlling for education and occupation, minority females received fewer training funds than any other group (Taylor, 1985:73). There is evidence to suggest that 'returns to institutionalised job training are greatest within the first three years of work with an employer', but in her study Taylor reports that the training provided to white males during this period was five times that provided to minority females (1985:77).

Training, of course, does more than simply enhance people's skills. It provides contacts and information, helps to establish networks among people, 'which facilitates their ability to produce as well as to make successful job shifts' (Taylor, 1985:76).

14 The importance of affirmative actions in the implementation strategies is clear. We want to change low-opportunity jobs, and most of the occupants of those jobs are members of the disadvantaged groups identified in our EEO legislation. The time spent in such jobs, almost by definition, has meant restricted access to advancement opportunites. Affirmative actions are geared to altering people's employment fortunes, not *because* they are members of disadvantaged groups, but because of what that membership has afforded them, in terms of job opportunities, in the past (Rosenbaum, 1984). We are, through affirmative actions, redressing the effects of past organisational practice. So it is reasonable to build into the process career development strategies and training in supervisory and administrative skills which ensure that women and members of the other disadvantaged groups get the skills and experiences they have not had access to in the past.

We are having to develop what Rosenbaum calls 'second chance' strategies, particularly for secretaries and keyboard workers who have been in their positions for a considerable time. One form this might take is what is called in a private sector firm 'gap training' (Chris McArthy, pers. comm.), whereby women who have been in low-opportunity jobs spend a certain number of days a month with a higher-level officer, learning the work of a different type of position in a supportive and non-threatening way, and becoming more rapidly promotable in the progress. Many such initiatives will have to be devised.

I conclude by commenting on a lesson we learn from the written assessments of work reorganisation efforts (see, for example, Robson, 1978). Participation of the workforce through their unions is critical if the changes are going to be more than token ones. If managers interpret the restructuring exercise as one which they control and one which is designed to give them greater control over workers, then conflict and disillusionment lie ahead. Organisational theorists and consultants have tended to reinforce the view that operators, or those below middle management, have little to contribute to knowledge about the workings of organisations. We know better than that, and success of the current initiatives depends upon the active involvement of the people who will be most affected by the changes: the occupants of the redesigned jobs.

7 EEO in the public sector: an agenda for the 1990s

While the development of 'people' resources is increasingly acknowledged to be an important aspect of the efficient and productive running of our agencies (e.g. Stace, 1987:54), what this actually means for the organisation of those resources is not always clear. There appears to be a tension, in practice, between strong guidance from Human Resources Management (HRM) executives in the organisation and the need to give line managers 'ownership' of their HRM practices (Stace, 1987:59). But, of course, the balance to be struck differs, depending on the broader context within which it occurs.

In some respects, paradoxically enough, the greater the sensitivity to EEO issues in the public sector, the greater the likelihood that one would find strong corporate guidance, combined with more progressive policies, at unit, branch or divisional level (see discussion of Kanter's work in chapter 5).

This chapter points to some of the EEO issues which will emerge during the 1990s in Australia and which will need careful and prolonged treatment before integration of the function into all agency decision-making processes can effectively occur. EEO cannot become a reality until agencies are staffed on sound and progressive principles of human resources management.

Of all the personnel systems likely to be implemented within public sector agencies, merit selection and performance assessment are the two which will play central roles in the determination of people's advancement opportunities and salary levels. Merit-based selections in an EEO context have been discussed widely, and I will not deal with them directly here.

Many initiatives within a corporate planning context will rely heavily on the results of some form of performance assessment. In a systematic HRM program, performance assessment results are used to make various related personnel decisions, dealing with promotion, transfer, redundancy, and training and development. Clearly, performance assessment will be important in performance- or merit-based payment systems (Geis, 1987:52; see also Halachmi and Holzer, 1987:81).

It is important, then, to look at the evidence of sex and race bias in performance assessment and related systems, and look at the efforts that have been made in other countries, particularly in the United States but also in Britain, to ensure that systematic bias is minimised in the design and implementation of such systems.

As we develop HRM systems that are, on the face of it, objective and fair, and as we collect more data on employment patterns required for the development of EEO programs, we are likely to witness more interest in processes of indirect discrimination within our agencies and more activity directed to removing it. Again, we can learn from experience in the United States and Britain about the ways in which we might reduce the incidence of indirect discrimination in rules and practices within our agencies, as well as in the HRM systems that we might develop.

An issue related to EEO programs that is likely to receive sustained attention during the 1990s is that of pay equity, particularly in so far as women's wages are seen as remaining lower on average than men's for reasons unrelated to skills and qualifications. There is scope for reducing the wage disparity through EEO programs, but we can also expect industrial activity around this issue by those who would argue that the EEO initiatives, particularly those directed at encouraging women into traditionally male-dominated work areas, do not address the problem of equitable remuneration for work performed in traditionally female-dominated occupations.

INDIRECT DISCRIMINATION

It is thirteen years since indirect discrimination was first regulated by anti-discrimination law in Australia (*Sex Discrimination Act* 1975 (SA)) and a shorter period of time since it has become more generally recognised as a form of discrimination, through its inclusion in other State legislation and the *Sex Discrimination Act* 1984 (Cwlth). The law is 'still in its infancy', as commentators put it when noting the thirteen years of 'meaningful experience' of EEO legislation in the US (McEnery and Lifter, 1987:64). In Australia during this time, only three cases of indirect discrimination have received judicial treatment (*Najdovska v. Australian Iron and Steel*, NSW Equal Opportunity Tribunal, 1985, NSW Court of Appeal, 1988; *The Australian Public Service Association v. The Australian Trade Commission*, Human Rights and Equal Opportunity Commission, 1988; *Styles v. The*

Secretary of the Department of Foreign Affairs and Trade and Anor, Federal Court of Australia, 1988).

We might expect the 1990s to be a significant decade for the development of a substantial body of case law on what is lawful and what is unlawful under the sections of Acts dealing with forms of indirect discrimination.

Hunter (1988) has produced a wide-ranging and thorough treatment of the concept of indirect discrimination in a research report written to clarify and explore the concept in order 'to encourage greater and more creative use of the legislative provisions'. 'The problem with indirect discrimination . . .', she says, 'is that it does not accord with popular conceptions of "discrimination". Thus an individual complaint-based system will not produce many complaints of indirect discrimination' (1988:19–20). 'Indirect discrimination' provisions indicate 'that a requirement or condition which is apparently neutral, or does not appear to have a greater impact on one group over another, may be open to challenge as being discriminatory' (Ronalds, 1987:99).

The definition provided in section 5(2) of the *Sex Discrimination Act* 1984 set out below contains four elements, all of which must be present in order to make out a case of indirect discrimination:

> For the purposes of this Act, a person (in this sub-section referred to as the 'discriminator') discriminates against another person (in this sub-section referred to as the 'aggrieved person') on the ground of the sex of the aggrieved person if the discriminator requires the aggrieved person to comply with a requirement or condition—
>
> (a)   with which a substantially higher proportion of persons of the opposite sex to the aggrieved person comply or are able to comply;
>
> (b)   which is not reasonable having regard to the circumstances of the case; and
>
> (c)   with which the aggrieved person does not or is not able to comply.

As Wilcox J put it in his judgment in the *Styles* case,

> discrimination against a group of people on account of some shared characteristic—such as sex, race, colour or age—often takes a subtle form. By reason of historical facts or ingrained attitudes, rules and practices which, upon their face, make no distinction between different groups of people—'facially neutral', in the American terminology—may have the effect of operating unfairly upon a particular group. In such a case a disadvantage may be visited upon members of that group which is not made the less real because it is indirect, unintended and even unwitting. (*Styles v. Department of Foreign Affairs and Trade*, 84 ALR 408 at 421)

A more colourful way of putting the same point was provided in the US Supreme Court case of 1971, *Griggs v. Duke Power Co.*, the seminal case which was to influence the development of legislation in Britain and in Australia, initially through the adoption of the concept of indirect discrimination in the South Australian *Sex Discrimination Act*. In this case, brought by a black employee, the Supreme Court held that the requirement of a high-school education or the passing of a standardised general intelligence test could not legally be used as a condition of employment in, or transfer to, jobs where the requirements were not shown to be job-related (Lubben et al., 1980:13):

> Congress has now provided that tests or criteria for employment or promotion may not provide equality of opportunity merely in the sense of the fabled offer of milk to the stork and the fox. On the contrary, Congress has now required that the posture and condition of the job-seeker be taken into account. It has — to resort again to the fable — provided that the vessel in which the milk is proffered be one all seekers can use. The Act proscribes not only overt discrimination but also practices that are fair in form, but discriminatory in operation.

The following sections illustrate some of the types of complaints of indirect discrimination that might emerge and reach the courts during the 1990s, based on cases that have been heard in Britain and the United States and on evaluations in the literature of what might constitute indirect discrimination in commonly found employment practices (see also Hunter, 1988:ch. 3). We would not expect as great a reliance on the courts as is found in America, particularly since we have an emphasis on conciliation in the first instance. Some of the more difficult cases, however, might be expected to find their way to the courts.

The first type includes complaints of indirect discrimination in access to employment opportunities which flow from the organisation of work, particularly from patterns of occupational segregation.

In organisations where the identification of promotion potential is restricted to categories of employees at grades above those at which most women are employed we have 'an example of an apparently unbiased policy being, in practice, discriminatory' (Ashridge Management College, 1980:145−6) since few women would be assessed for promotion potential.

If situations such as this one were to be taken up as instances of indirect discrimination, the implications for the organisation of work would be far-reaching. Areas where career paths are lacking and within which the jobs are predominantly held by women are common. Where an 'internal incentive structure' provided 'to encourage the development of firm-specific skills' is not available, for example, to female operators to the same extent that it is to male operators within the same enterprise (Curtain, 1987:28), an argument that this constitutes indirect discrimination might be put. Of course, these are precisely the situations affirmative action programs are designed to deal with by the removal of unnecessary, arbitrary and artificial barriers to employment opportunities. They are, as well, the conditions that award restructuring is expected to alter, a point to which I shall return.

The second type includes complaints which result from the application of apparently neutral HRM systems — such as job evaluation and performance assessment systems — but which have race and/or sex bias built into them. These systems usually reflect organisational values and norms. Indeed, performance assessment systems can be used effectively to signal a change in organisational values, something which could be kept in mind when setting them up within an EEO environment: 'when an organization wants to change the behavior of its employees or introduce a new set of procedures, it can simultaneously communicate this to employees and underline its importance by including the areas as items on formal performance appraisals' (Brinkerhoff and Kanter, 1980:5).

In the English case of *Watches of Switzerland v. Savell* (1983), an industrial tribunal found the employer's vague and subjective promotion procedure, administered by male managers, had a disproportionately adverse effect on women. The very subjectivity of the process, which lacked any guidelines or written criteria for promotion, was found to be potentially discriminatory against women. The tribunal found that the procedure 'contained no, or no adequate mechanism to prevent subconscious bias against women' (Hunter, 1988:47).

Some of the instances of race and sex bias in performance assessment schemes referred to later illustrate how the schemes indirectly discriminate on grounds of race and sex. Phillips (1986) found more subtle instances of indirect discrimination operating in performance assessment processes, and other instances are given below in chapter 10.

One of the qualities frequently regarded as evidence of leadership ability is 'the ability to persuade others', a reasonable criterion on the face of it. But how is it to be assessed in a sex-neutral way? Phillips describes an assessment centre procedure where

a group of six young management trainees were asked to agree to a list of the most significant inventions of recent times ... All the men in the group compiled lists which, when compared, appeared to be very similar. They had thought of such things as the silicon chip and aerodynamics. The only woman in the group had a totally different list which included items such as the contraceptive pill ... When the final consensus was made up it did not include a single item suggested by the female candidate. Further, she did not get a positive rating from the assessors because her performance did not demonstrate an ability to be persuasive in a discussion. (1986:5)

In addition to these two types of complaints — that is, those flowing from the organisation of work and those resulting from the application of apparently neutral HRM systems — there are those arising from the different circumstances under which women, or people from non-English-speaking backgrounds, or people with a physical disability, or Aboriginal people, undertake employment.

The English case of *Holmes v. The Home Office* (1984) related to a woman taking maternity leave for her first and second child and on both occasions requesting part-time work when she returned from maternity leave. The department refused on the grounds that no part-time positions were available within her grade. Ms Holmes claimed that the refusal to make part-time work available constituted sex discrimination, and an industrial tribunal and the Employment Appeals Tribunal agreed:

> The requirement to work full-time indirectly discriminated against women and the Home Office had failed to justify the requirement imposed on Ms Holmes. Whether a requirement to work full-time is or is not justifiable is a matter for the industrial tribunal to decide on the facts of each particular case. (Janner, 1988:336)

The situation of women of non-English-speaking background provides other examples:

> A requirement that leading hands or supervisors be able to speak English ... may have a disproportionately adverse effect on the women in that group, since migrant women have less access to English classes than migrant men because of their childcare and domestic responsibilities ... An employer's refusal to allow time off work to attend English classes could, in some cases, amount to an indirect and unreasonable bar to women's promotional opportunities. (Hunter, 1988:52)

The extension of affirmative action into the private sector combined with a greater awareness of the availability of provisions dealing with indirect discrimination will feed into each other over time with repercussions for public sector practice. As Hunter points out, 'the greater availability of statistical data as a result of affirmative action legislation should facilitate the establishment of indirect discrimination complaints' (1988:135) and 'the judicious pursuit of indirect discrimination complaints under anti-discrimination legislation might give some much-needed impetus to the development of adequate affirmative action programs' (1988:226).

PERFORMANCE ASSESSMENT

Many of the concerns EEO practitioners have with existing perform-ance assessment systems are shared by people commenting on such systems from the point of view of human resources management. The general concern with invalid, unreliable and unfair results has broad-ened, however, to a concern with the systematic race and sex bias effects that have been identified. Much of the relevant data has been assembled in America, where more attention has been paid to these issuses than is yet the case in Australia, probably because of stricter statutory requirements and the expense involved in non-compliance. It has meant a burst of literature treating the subject of how you make your system 'court-proof' (e.g. Lazer, 1976; Schneier, 1978; Klasson et al., 1980; Lubben et al., 1980; Feild and Holley, 1982; Richards, 1984; Burchett and De Meuse, 1985; Edwards and Sproull, 1985; Goddard, 1985; Martin et al., 1986–87; Sims et al., 1987). There has been similar comment in the Australian literature, but more in anticipation of what is to come than as a reflection of the existing situation (e.g. Lansbury, 1981:xvi; McCarthy and Stone, 1986:224; Bond, 1987).

Feild and Holley (1982) studied the effects of thirteen charact-eristics of assessment systems on the verdicts rendered in 66 US employment discrimination cases (where 31 ruled in favour of the plaintiff and 35 in favour of the defendant). Four characteristics of the systems were found to distinguish judgments for the plaintiffs from judgments for the defendants. Successful defendants' assessment systems tended to possess the following characteristics:

1 individuals responsible for evaluating employees were given specific written instructions on how to complete the assessments;

2 assessments were made using a system that was behaviour-oriented rather than trait-oriented;

3 the content of the assessment system was based on thorough job analysis; and

4 the results of the assessments were reviewed with each employee. (Feild and Holley, 1982:398)

Bond (1987:45), citing another review of American court cases (Kleiman and Durham, 1981), lists the traits which have been held 'to be subjective and subject to conscious or unconscious bias': adaptability, bearing, demeanour, manner, maturity, drive, social behaviour, leadership ability, experience, general intelligence, general business acumen, past job performance, personal appearance, co-operation, dependability and stability (see also Livy, 1988a:180, 194).

It is difficult to persuade many managers that such traits as drive, dependability, leadership ability and so on are irrelevant as criteria on which to assess people particularly if the results of the assessment are to be used for promotion or transfer decisions.

But if the court rulings and the commentaries in the literature are any guide, it would appear that, if characteristics such as these are relevant to job performance, then they require 'unambiguous, consistently applied, well-communicated, job-relevant illustrations and definitions' (Schneier et al., 1986:39).

In Australia, many performance assessment schemes rate people on traits such as these, without the checks and balances needed to 'ensure that arbitrary, capricious or ill-intended judgements ... could not operate' (Bond, 1987:45, citing Kleiman and Durham, 1981:117). Such schemes would not, if challenged, satisfy the requirements of the anti-discrimination and affirmative action Acts (see McCarthy and Stone, 1986:230).

A reason for preferring behaviour- rather than trait-oriented approaches, of course, is to minimise the potential for bias involved in the process (see Livy, 1988a). And there is an additional set of arguments from an EEO perspective, because research findings in the literature suggest that the greater the ambiguity in the criteria used, the more likely it is that race and sex bias will be found.

In general, the experts agree, the more ambiguity and uncertainty there are in determining what is required for good performance in a job, the more likely raters are to favour performers like themselves (Kane and Lawler, 1979:454), resulting, while most raters are white males, in sex bias (e.g. Nieva and Gutek, 1980) and race bias (e.g. Kraiger and Ford, 1985).

Moreover, there is evidence that ratees are assessed according to different performance criteria, depending on their sex and race. One study investigated whether different criteria are used to evaluate white and black managers' performance. More particularly, the researchers sought to discover whether 'social behavioral' skills tend to be more heavily weighted in evaluating the overall job performance of black ratees versus white ratees (Cox and Nkomo, 1986:104–5). On finding that they were, the researchers concluded that

> a white manager may be overly concerned with the social behavior of a black subordinate as a test of the extent to which the latter is perceived to 'fit in' with the established social norms of the organisation. Assimilation to these requirements therefore becomes a major part of the black manager's 'performance'. (1986:104)

Two cases which reached the courts in America illustrate the importance of developing valid measures of performance where the assessment systems are used for making decisions about promotions, transfers and lay-offs.

> In *Rome v. General Motors Corp.* the Fifth Circuit Court of Appeals concluded that the lack of blacks who were promoted or transferred resulted from the reliance upon all-white supervisory recommendations which were based on subjective and vague standards ...
> In *Brito v. Sia Co.* the Tenth Circuit Court of Appeals ruled that Sia had violated Title VII [of the *Civil Rights Act* of 1964] when, on the basis of poor performance ratings, it laid off several Spanish surnamed employees ... The Court concluded that the assessments were not [based] on any identifiable objective criteria ... (Klasson et al., 1980:78)

The findings for female ratees are similar, in those situations where there is ambiguity in or uncertainty about the requirements for effective job performance:

> the level of inference required of the evaluator appears to be directly related to the occurrence of pro-male bias. Bias tends to be found in situations where inferences about the causality of performance are called for, where extrapolation from available information to future contexts is required (i.e., in selection and promotion), and where there is ambiguity concerning the focal female or the evaluation criteria. (Nieva and Gutek, 1980:273).

In *Nord v. US Steel Corp.* the Eleventh Circuit Court of Appeal found in favour of the plaintiff in a case which 'involved a female sales-service clerk who received written evaluations of "good as most" or "above average" over a period of six years' (Martin et al., 1986–87:379). She received her first adverse evaluation after she had twice requested promotion. The court noted a number of characteristics of the promotion process that indicated a 'built-in mechanism for sex discrimination'. Among them were:

> all management personnel and supervisors were male, the principal factor in receiving a promotion was a recommendation from a supervisor ... there were no established standards or procedures regarding promotions, and employees were not given information regarding the necessary qualifications for promotions. (Cited in Martin et al., 1986–87:379–80).

Cases such as these led Edwards and Sproull (1985:17) to conclude that 'companies that underutilize minority group members or women while promoting men, based on supervisors' subjective recommendations, are sitting ducks for litigation'.

The answer to the problem of race and sex bias in assessment systems is not to attempt to make all evaluations 'objective', as Lenney and associates imply when they say that providing clear evaluation criteria is a relatively simple and inexpensive technique which 'can be applied in business, professional, and academic settings' (1983:327). Rather, the answer lies in accepting the inevitability of subjective judgments within performance assessment processes, as in merit selection processes (see chapter 4; see also Burton, 1988), the more so where performance being assessed is in jobs with discretion built into them as to how one can perform effectively.

Courts in America have not ruled that subjective evaluations are illegal:

> the legitimacy of the articulated reason for the employment decision is subject to particularly close scrutiny where the evaluation is subjective and the evaluators themselves are not members of the protected minority ... The ultimate issue in each case is whether the subjective criteria were used to disguise subjective action. (*Grano v. Department of Development of the City of Columbus*, cited in Martin et al., 1986−87:392)

But the courts have, from time to time, indicated their preference, in situations where subjective evaluations are relied on, for the provision of appeal and discussion rights to the employee:

> If established procedures have given an employee a reasonable opportunity to inspect the supervisory evaluations in his or her file, to challenge allegedly inaccurate materials, and to have such materials corrected or removed, and if the organization gives its employees adequate notice that these rights may be exercised, then it may rely in good faith on such evaluations in making subsequent employment decisions without violating Title VII (*Stoller v. Marsh*, cited in Martin et al., 1986−87:394; see also Edwards and Sproull, 1985:24; Bond, 1987:45)

Part of the answer to the problem of sex and race bias lies in adequate training of raters (Richards, 1984; Bond, 1987). However, training provided for raters often does not include training in the area of differential treatment of different ratee groups, and specifically the danger of race and sex bias in evaluations (Dipboye, 1985:123; Kraiger and Ford, 1986:61). In addition, it is essential to have included in raters' (that is, supervisors' and managers') own performance assessments the attainment of EEO objectives (Brinkerhoff and Kanter, 1980; Edwards and Sproull, 1985; Seear, 1988) to provide an incentive to 'get it right'.

In America the Uniform Guidelines on Employee Selection Procedures developed by the EEOC and the US Department of Labor (EEOC, 1978)−'a fourteen thousand-word catalog of do's and don'ts and questions and answers for hiring and promotion' (Schuler and Youngblood, 1986:159)−have 'essentially gained the force of law in recent years' (Burchett and De Meuse, 1985:32; see also

Lubben et al., 1980:13) and are regarded as applicable not only to selection processes but to performance assessments when results from these are used in making employment decisions.

Similarly, in the United Kingdom, codes of practice have been developed by the Equal Opportunities Commission (1985) and by the Commission for Racial Equality (1983). Again, they do not have the force of law but they have been approved by Parliament and 'the courts or tribunals can take them into account in determining legal issues. This means, in effect, that the many parts of the Codes are indirectly legally enforceable' (Greenhalgh, 1987:427; see also Equal Opportunities Review, 1988b:17).

We can envisage the development of codes of practice and guidelines by the central EEO and AA agencies in Australia to cover the practices identified as critical in the determination of people's access to employment opportunities. These are likely, in the event of complaints being brought before tribunals and the courts, to guide the decisions that are made, and in due course to assume a legal status.

EMPLOYMENT AND WAGE DISCRIMINATION

It is commonly believed that Australian women are doing all right on the wages front. The female—male wage ratio is better than in many countries, such as the United States, Canada and Britain. The benefits, to women, of the 1969 and 1972 equal pay rulings of the Australian Conciliation and Arbitration Commission, and the decision in 1974 to extend the minimum wage to females, are clear. For full-time workers the ratio of female—male average weekly earnings was 0.65 in 1972 and 0.79 in 1977; it remained, however, at 0.79 in 1987 (Australian Bureau of Statistics *Average Weekly Earnings* (February Series, Cat. No. 6302.0).

This relatively healthy ratio has given rise to the view that women's wage rates in Australia can only improve, now, by moving women across a wider range of industries and occupations, and further up occupational and organisational hierarchies. It is argued that EEO or affirmative action programs hold the key to ending the wage discrepancy.

One can accept the common sense of this response to the situation. Women are overrepresented in many low-paying occupations. If they were to work in higher-paid occupations, then by definition women's average wage rates would rise.

But apart from other major problems in this argument, some of which were stated in chapter 3 (and see Game, 1984; National Pay Equity Coalition, 1988), it denies an important fact. It is not just that women are in low-paying occupations: such occupations are frequently low-paying because women work in them (see, for example, Rosenbaum, 1985; Pfeffer and Blake-Davis, 1987; Strober and Arnold, 1987). EEO programs are limited in their capacity to deal with this fundamental problem. It is this evident fact — that the work women do is devalued because women do it — which is the prime target of pay equity strategies (see chapter 11).

Effective EEO programs could contribute to the reduction in wage disparities by opening up advancement opportunities for the target groups. But this is not to say, as opponents of 'comparable worth' in the US have done (e.g. Livernash, 1980; Bellak et al., 1983), that the wage disparity between women and men in the workforce can be dealt with entirely through EEO initiatives.

It is worth looking, then, at what can be achieved and why other activity, particularly in the industrial arena, is likely to continue around the pay equity issue in Australia through the 1990s.

There is certainly scope for some progress in reducing the wage disparity by asking the following questions and dealing with the answers through EEO strategies:

1 Are men and women of equal qualifications and experience appointed at different salary levels within the same classification?

2 Within the same classification or work level, are men and women streamed according to whether the job is more routine or more challenging?

3 Are men and women who apply for entry positions in the same organisation placed in different classifications, such as females in the clerical ranks and males in the officer ranks?

4 Do employers give men and women different degrees of encouragement to attain qualifications or experiences necessary for advancement?

5 Are women with lower formal educational qualifications than men recruited and placed in a lower classification regardless of job content demands or the qualities and skills required to perform in the different positions?

6 Do prevailing definitions of merit or efficiency contain elements of gender bias?

7 Are career paths for men and women in the same classification different from each other? For example, are females put onto machine work or data input work, while males are given work recognised as important for advancement?

8 Are low-opportunity jobs, consisting of routine and repetitive work, designed specifically for women in the belief that women are better at concentrating on detailed or fiddly work and/or are not likely to want a career?

9 Are women precluded from taking up positions which are used for developmental purposes because their incumbency blocks the advancement opportunities of males?

10 Is the training offered to women of the kind that makes them better performers in their current positions, while the training offered to men is of the kind that makes them more promotable?

All of these matters ought, in theory, to be covered by EEO programs in order to enhance the employment opportunities of women; if they were they would have an effect on relative rates of pay.

Another way in which EEO programs can contribute to the reduction of wage discrimination is through strategies designed to ensure that job evaluation systems are free of gender bias. I have dealt with this issue extensively in *Women's Worth* (see chapter 11), and have indicated that little effort has been put into dealing with gender bias in these systems in Australia to date. This is unlike the situations in countries where 'equal pay for work of equal value' legislation exists and has prompted official concern to develop systems free of gender bias (for example Canada, countries within the European Economic Community, and various states of America).

What emerges over and over again in the literature, both here and overseas (see, for example, Treiman and Hartmann, 1981; Rubenstein, 1984; Steinberg and Haignere, 1985; Burton et al., 1987; Hyman, 1987), is how attributes women bring to work, such as manual dexterity and social skills, are not remunerated because they are regarded as female qualities, whereas qualities attributed to males, such as physical strength, are valued and remunerated. Moreover, because of the sex-segregated nature of the workforce, a situation has developed where the skills and qualities required in female-dominated jobs are less likely than those required in male-dominated jobs to have found their place in the list of criteria used to determine job worth. Because they have not been acknowledged, they have not been remunerated.

It is likely that the use of job evaluation systems for pay-setting will continue to increase in both the public and private sectors in the coming years. Several different systems will be used, some more responsive than others to the possibility of gender bias. Skill-based payment systems (paying the person for the range of skills accumulated, regardless of whether the higher skills are used all of the time) will compete with the more traditional job evaluation systems based on the demands of the job. But they are all methods of systematising pay-setting procedures, and it is imperative that we develop our knowledge and understanding of the ways in which sex and, conceivably, race bias might enter them.

The pay equity issue is reemerging within the context of award restructuring and the current wage-fixing principles. In 1988 a group called the National Pay Equity Coalition made a submission in the National Wage Case. We now have a 15-year-old tradition of women's organisations appearing before the Conciliation and Arbitration Commission with arguments for building into the wage-fixing processes better mechanisms for determining the relative work value of jobs held predominantly by women.

The National Pay Equity Coalition's submission raised the implications for women of the award-restructuring process, in relation to their employment opportunities and their relative wages. It was noted, for example, that unless women's existing skills and responsibilities were adequately accounted for when decisions about access to training and retraining and multiskilling were made, they would remain disadvantaged in their career paths and remuneration. Further, when new classifications were set up and their relative work value assessed, it was argued that unless the knowledge we have about how gender bias affects such assessments was applied, female-dominated classifications, once again, would be underpaid relative to male-dominated classifications.

The submission recommended that:

> The Commission should require that award restructuring and training packages put forward under national wage guidelines include an equal opportunity assessment of the measures proposed. The equity assessment must include a skills audit of existing and proposed classifications, carried out in a non-discriminatory manner, and which recognises the knowledge, skills and experience of female workers in existing classifications, and takes account of job demands. The equity assessment should also establish whether access to training and promotion and movement from one classification to another is equally accessible to all workers, and how the proposed changes address inequities in the positions of males and females in the workforce. (National Pay Equity Coalition, 1988:5)

Thus the commission was requested to monitor the award-restructuring process, and one might expect that this call will be repeated when the commission meets to review the process.

At the agency level, there is likely to be more active involvement of EEO officers in the work reorganisation that results from restructuring agreements. We can also expect more active involvement in these processes on the part of the central AA and EEO agencies. An example of this is provided by the Affirmative Action Agency's recommendations on the ways in which the Metals Award restructure should occur in practice (Affirmative Action Agency, 1988), recommendations based on arguments similar to those presented in the National Pay Equity Coalition's submission.

Progress in EEO in the 1990s will be influenced by the increased emphasis on efficiency and accountability now permeating the public sector. Changes in the structure of organisations, the changing relationships of central agencies to individual departments and authorities, and the emphasis on productivity-geared HRM systems could deliver more effective EEO programs. However, unless applied with care in the workplace, such changes could actively frustrate the aims of EEO programs and limit the extension of employment opportunities for the target groups.

From the viewpoint of efficiency and effectiveness one can see, and seize, the opportunity to integrate EEO principles into the changes that are presently occurring and to free our human resources management systems from indirect and systematic race and sex bias.

But the EEO agenda is not the sole preserve of EEO interest groups and practitioners. Other people have interests which will be brought to bear on the issues in practice. This means that the integration of EEO principles into other organisational decision-making processes will be uneven and contested. The aspects of EEO activity outlined above — legal challenges to forms of indirect discrimination, the identification of race and sex bias in HRM systems, and moves to counter wage discrimination through EEO programs and industrial activity — are, in my view, likely to receive increased attention over the next decade in Australia.

PART III
Valuing Women's Work

8 Gender bias in job evaluation

This chapter is concerned with the use of job evaluation schemes as a basis for classifying jobs into wage or salary grades. The use of such schemes within an enterprise is an employment practice that requires review under section 8 (1) (f) of the *Affirmative Action Act*. Under the Act, employers are expected to identify and eliminate practices which, directly or indirectly, discriminate against women. The requirements of this section are supported, of course, by the Commonwealth *Sex Discrimination Act* 1984.

The Act gives effect to certain provisions of the *Convention on the Elimination of All Forms of Discrimination Against Women*. Article 11, paragraph 1 (d), gives women 'the right to equal remuneration, including benefits, and to equal treatment in respect of work of equal value ...'.

It would appear, then, that the use of formal job evaluation schemes within enterprises would need to be non-discriminatory to comply with the provisions of the *Sex Discrimination Act*.

JOB EVALUATION: A GENERAL BACKGROUND

Job evaluation may be defined simply as an attempt to determine and compare the demands which the normal performance of particular jobs makes on normal workers without taking account of the individual abilities or performance of the workers concerned (ILO, 1960:8)

The result of the job evaluation comparisons is a ranking of jobs within the one enterprise, an internal hierarchy of job 'worth' which, in one way or another, is used for pay-setting. Whether variations in individual performance in similarly classified jobs are also taken into account in pay-setting is 'something entirely different from the rating of the job' (ILO, 1960:8).

The usual reason for the introduction of a formal job evaluation scheme is to systematise a wage or salary-setting process that appears to have become haphazard, or has developed in ways that no longer appear equitable or sensible. It may accompany other organisational change, signalling perhaps a shift in corporate philosophy.

Job evaluation methods can be divided into two broad types.[1] The first consists of those which use qualitative methods to assess whole jobs against other jobs, either by comparing them to one another and ranking them (the ranking method), or by allocating them to a grade within a predetermined set of hierarchically ordered grades (the classification method). These grades are broadly described in line with the duties, responsibilities and skill requirements of positions within them.

The second type, with which this chapter is concerned, consists of quantitative (or analytic) methods. A set of 'compensable' factors is chosen, factors such as the skill, effort, and responsibility required for competent performance in the job. The most widely used quantitative method is the points-rating method (Livy, 1988b:228). Job evaluation schemes using this method define a set of factors and assign scores to each job for each factor. The scores for each job are added up to obtain an overall rating of the job in relation to other jobs covered by the scheme. These scores are referred to as a measure of the relative 'worth' or 'value' of the job to the organisation.

Job evaluation systems have received a lot of attention in other countries in recent years. This has been the result of legislative and other initiatives addressing issues relating to discrimination in employment. In the United States wage discrimination claims have been made under the *Equal Pay Act* 1963 and Title VII of the *Civil Rights Act* 1964. In America the 'comparable worth' doctrine has generated widespread application of quantitative job evaluation methods to determine the relative value of predominantly male and predominantly female occupations (see Cook, 1985; 1986). In countries within the European Economic Community, such as the United Kingdom, and other countries such as Canada, which have equal pay for work of equal value legislation,[2] a preference is expressed for the use of quantitative rather than 'whole job' schemes to determine equal pay claims.

Many enterprises in Australia use or are introducing quantitative job evaluation schemes (all major banks, many higher education institutions, some State and local governments, insurance companies, and many other private sector firms). Different schemes operate and different coverage exists. In some enterprises only professional, technical and managerial positions are covered; in others, the scheme covers clerical positions or award wages staff although there may be an intention to extend coverage upwards. Enterprises may use different schemes for different categories of employees, or extend the use of one scheme to cover a wider range of employees.

There is no such thing as an 'objective' job evaluation system. Despite the apparent scientific basis of the techniques which use numerical measures to evaluate job worth, the literature on job evaluation techniques is consistent in its emphasis on the subjective judgments that form part of the evaluation process (Livy, 1975:126; Livernash, 1980:9; Thomason, 1980:45; Walker and Bowey, 1982:89; Rubenstein, 1984:96; Livy, 1988b:243). What a properly designed and implemented job evaluation scheme can do, though, is 'promote the systematic and consistent application of considered judgments about the relative worth of jobs' (Gillett, 1987:2).

The value base to the job evaluation process is recognised by the consultants of the firms which offer the systems. They stress the importance of reaching consensus within the evaluation committees set up by the client organisation. They acknowledge the role of the organisational 'culture' in determining the internal ranking of positions. Through the evaluation of an initial representative set of 'benchmark' positions,[3] consensus is reached on what the values of the organisation are. From there, with adequate training in analysing and evaluating positions, consistency in evaluations is possible.

But consensus can be arrived at in different ways and it might be more apparent than real. The value system of the organisation might reflect some perspectives and points of view and not others. Female occupants of positions relatively low in organisational hierarchies may not be in a position to put their views on the relative value of different kinds of work as strongly as other organisational participants.

Furthermore, despite the fact that it is jobs and not people supposedly being evaluated, the sex of the typical incumbent appears to have a significant influence on the perception of the nature of the work and thus the determination of its value. As Treiman says, 'the evidence of sex stereotyping in job-related contexts is certainly strong enough to suggest the likelihood that sex stereotyping will pervade the evaluation of jobs strongly identified with one sex or the other' (1979:45).

We must, therefore, acknowledge the possibility for gender bias to enter. This is usually thought to be particularly likely at two points in the process: in the writing of the job description and in the evaluation of the description (see below). But we need to address, too, the possibility of gender bias being built into the design of job evaluation schemes.

THE DESIGN OF SCHEMES: THE CHOICE, DEFINITION AND WEIGHTING OF COMPENSABLE FACTORS

The factors measured in jobs are the 'compensable' factors — 'job characteristics that are regarded as contributing to the overall worth of the job' (Treiman, 1979:6). The ranking of jobs under a job evaluation scheme is highly dependent on which factors are selected for measurement and how heavily each factor is weighted. 'One set of factors and factor weights may produce a particular ordering of jobs while a different set of factors or a different weighting of factors may produce quite a different ordering' (Treiman, 1979:6). Because of the sex-segregated nature of the workforce, the choice of factors and the weightings given to them can have a significant effect on the relative rankings of predominantly female-held positions and predominantly male-held positions.

The Equal Opportunities Commission in Britain (1985b:8—9) sets out the changes in relative scores for a maintenance fitter and a company nurse, depending on factor definition and relative weightings given to the different factors. On a 'discriminatory' set of factors (one which, among other things, emphasises experience in the job rather than training, physical effort rather than mental effort, and does not emphasise responsibility for people) the fitter receives 64 points to the nurse's 22. On a 'less biased' set of factors (which emphasises, among other things, basic knowledge, complexity of tasks, training, and includes mental effort and responsibility for people) the fitter recieves 53 points, the nurse 54 (Equal Opportunities Commission, 1985b:8—9; see also Treiman, 1984:86—89).

A further issue relating to the factors is the consequence of different 'operational indicators' of the factors being measured. For example, how is skill defined and measured? What are the effects of measuring skill through experience, and measuring it through formal educational requirements? The decision will have an effect on the relative ranking of female-dominated and male-dominated jobs, as the above example makes clear (see also Treiman and Hartmann, 1981:75).

Treiman suggests that the choice of operational indicators appears to be oriented to predominantly male jobs. He provides the following examples:

> Effort is usually measured by strength requirements rather than fatigue levels, with the consequence that predominantly male blue-collar jobs will almost invariably score higher on the effort factor than will predominantly female blue-collar jobs, even if they are equally fatiguing for the average worker. As another example, manual skill factors stress ability to handle tools rather than manual dexterity, which has the effect of downgrading fine assembly work, done largely by women. In office and executive

plans, interpersonal skill factors stress negotiating rather than counselling or conciliating roles. Responsibility is defined in terms of supervising, or budgetary control, rather than in terms of organising. (1979:32)

He concludes that 'insofar as true differences . . . between predominantly male and predominantly female jobs go unmeasured because inappropriate operational indicators are used, the resulting job worth scores will be biased' (1979:33).

In women's process production work manual dexterity, accuracy and concentration have not been recognised to the same extent as physical effort and strength factors. And in clerical work, working conditions are frequently not given any weighting at all. It has been assumed that clerical workers operate in clean, safe and pleasant environments and that the work they perform is not hazardous or particularly stressful.

The measurement of the human relations or social skills component of jobs and of the accountability factor in job evaluation schemes has been widely criticised by those who are concerned with developing systems free of gender bias (see, for example, Greenwood, 1984:460; Remick, 1984a:96-97; Steinberg and Haignere, 1985:17, 20). As well, systems where 'double-counting' is possible — where a job characteristic, such as number of people supervised, can be considered under two or more headings, or where one factor is measured as a proportion of another — can be criticised for introducing the possibility of greater error. The effects of any under- or over-evaluation of the factor used as a basis for the calculation are compounded when that factor enters the calculation twice (see Burton et al., 1987:89; Hyman, 1987:12).

COLLECTING AND RECORDING INFORMATION ABOUT JOBS

Whether job occupants are filling in a questionnaire about their job, or a job analyst is preparing position descriptions from information gained through observation and interviews with the job holders and their supervisors, problems can emerge which lead to discriminatory evaluations[4].

Supervisors are, in fact, relied on heavily for information about jobs. Yet Treiman reports that clerical and secretarial jobs, in particular, are not well understood by supervisors. Since 'one of the typical responsibilities of a secretary is to take care of administrative detail without bothering the boss', the latter is probably unable to give a complete and accurate description of the tasks performed (1979:39).

When women respond to questions about their work, it appears that they respond to the 'cues' around them, and are liable to under-estimate the complexity, training time, or other dimensions of the demands of their jobs. The implementation of the system needs to take into account the possibility that lower-level workers are likely to reflect the status of their job in their description of it, and women more so than men, given the evidence of their 'self-deprecating' as against men's 'self-enhancing' job descriptions (McArthur, 1985:61; see also Remick, 1984b:107).

It may be that the use of sex-congruent words — words to describe activities that appear appropriate considering the sex of those carry-ing out those activities — involves a consistent difference in the ways jobs are described, and a subsequent difference in the evaluation of the jobs. Some examples of this are provided in *Women's Worth* (Burton et al., 1987). The researchers found, for example, that when contact with other organisations was a central feature of the position, it was described in very different terms for men's jobs and for women's jobs. For women's positions, interpersonal skills, patience, tact and common sense were important; for men, the fostering and promotion of a good image for the organisation were important. In relationships with suppliers, a man was required to negotiate and liaise, a woman was required to show good judgment (1987:59—60).

The research also identified different patterns of language use in the position descriptions. The passive voice was employed frequently in the position descriptions of female-held jobs to describe the carry-ing out of tasks, rendering the job holders less central to, and less active in, the work which was being described. The findings sup-ported those of another study, which found that 'job descriptions for white male jobs ... tend to be more specific, task-oriented, and use language which is aimed at and tracks the language used by the ... job evaluation system' (King and Hoffman, 1984:98), and that women's jobs are undervalued 'in part because their job descriptions are broad and general and because they are not constructed to earn higher points' (1984:98).

THE EVALUATION PROCESS

Qualities and skills frequently overlooked in the assessment of women's work have been detailed extensively in the literature. There is evidence to suggest that evaluators might overlook the following features of women's jobs:

- fine motor movement skills such as rapid finger dexterity;
- special body coordination or expert use of fingers and hands;
- coordinating (as against supervising);

- protecting confidentiality;
- record keeping;
- working office machines;
- language skills;
- interruptions and doing many tasks at once;
- communication stress;
- stress from concentration;
- stress from multiple role demands (being asked to do work quickly and to provide better service to several people);
- responding to complaints from the public;
- caring for people. (adapted from Steinberg and Haignere, 1985: 18−19)

They may overlook the communication skills of receptionists − but not the manual skills of machinery repairmen.
They may overlook the effort of lifting heavy patients − but not the lifting of heavy objects.
They may overlook the amount of responsibility involved in the education of children − but not the responsibility for finances and equipment.
They may overlook the stressful working conditions of looking after people with serious mental health problems − but not the noise of machinery. (Ontario Women's Directorate, 1988:15; see also Remick, 1984b:107)

Many women are employed for their 'maturity' and/or skills developed within the household. But these are not recognised as equivalent to the training and experience which can be measured and/or documented for their male counterparts, even though it is for these qualities and skills that the women are employed.

Overlooking women's job characteristics is frequently the result of job analysts and evaluators regarding job-related skills as qualities intrinsic to being a woman (Steinberg and Haignere, 1985:13−14; see also Burton et al., 1987:102).

THE TYPES OF 'BIAS' IDENTIFIED IN THE TWO STEPS OF JOB DESCRIPTION AND EVALUATION OF JOBS[5]

Availability bias

This refers to 'a tendency to describe the frequency of certain job-related activities according to their ease of retrieval from memory'

(McArthur, 1985:55). For example, a supervisor is likely to over-estimate the job element of typing in clerk-typist and secretarial position descriptions. It is more evident an activity than, for example, the quieter activity of composing literate letters.

Typing, clerical and secretarial jobs, predominantly performed by women, provide excellent examples of this form of bias and point to the importance of position description writers and job evaluation committee members being familiar with the work involved. Comments from committee members make this clear: 'a trained monkey could do it', 'it's just monkey stuff: you follow your nose', 'she's just typing', 'she just rings up'.[6]

> It has been pointed out that clerk-typists have frequently been regarded as mainly engaging in mechanical operations. However, when workers thoroughly familiar with the job [analyse or] evaluate it, mental and interpersonal job requirements may emerge — such as, 'ability to handle a number of tasks at one time', 'ability to proofread by self', 'ability to keep information confidential' and 'getting information from others on their needs' (Rubenstein, 1984:97)

Halo effect bias

This refers to the process whereby 'people who are labelled "good" on some important dimension are surrounded with a positive aura, or "halo", which causes other positive qualities to be ascribed to them. Conversely, people who are labelled as "bad" on some important dimensions are perceived as having a number of other negative qualities' (McArthur, 1985:57–58). This happens with jobs as well as with people. A highly responsible position might be perceived as requiring considerable technical knowledge. Halo effects 'make valued jobs seem even more valuable, and less valued jobs seem even less valuable' (Steinberg and Haignere, 1985:22).

The existence of such an effect suggests that the position description and the evaluation of it may be influenced by the job's status or its assumed pay. Low-status jobs may be regarded as low in worth regardless of actual job content, which may be perceived through a negative halo. It was noted earlier that different words might be used for public contact work, depending on whether it was performed by men or women, and this could lead to one job appearing more responsible, and more important, than another. Steinberg and Haignere call this a 'gender halo', which they say is 'characterized, in the extreme, by statements such as 'this job is performed by women, therefore, it must involve few skills ... or little responsibility ... or good working conditions (1985:22).

Expectancy bias and relationship to sex of job occupant

Expectancy bias refers to 'a tendency to describe a job with whatever characteristics are culturally expected for that job ... The result might be that job descriptions reflect at least in part social stereotypes rather than the true nature of the job' (McArthur, 1985:60).

Some studies have found a direct effect of the sex of the job occupant on evaluations. For example, McArthur and Obrant conducted an experiment using a videotaped depiction of several jobs and found that 'when jobs were depicted with male incumbents, analysts rated them as being relatively more critical to the company's assets and operations, as involving more responsibility, and as having relatively less structure ... than the same jobs depicted with female incumbents' (McArthur, 1985:62). The same research found that jobs depicted with female incumbents were rated by analysts as meriting relatively lower wages than the same jobs depicted with male incumbents (McArthur, 1985:63).

Influence of current pay rates

> The substantial influence of institutional and traditional arrangements makes it impossible to view current wage rates as set solely by the free play of neutral forces operating in an entirely open market, no matter how attractive such a theoretical formulation may be (Treiman and Hartmann, 1981:x).

Grams and Schwab (1985) conducted a study in which pay rates for jobs were manipulated to discover whether reported pay level for the job significantly influenced the evaluation of the job. Finding that it did, they commented that if evaluation judgments are influenced by current or market wages that are themselves biased against jobs in which women predominate, then such a bias can produce relatively deflated evaluations for jobs held predominantly by women (Grams and Schwab, 1985:288; see also Elizur, 1987:196).

But since pay rates reflect status hierarchies, and have the force of custom and tradition behind them, we could not expect the use of a job evaluation system to lead to radical alterations in the internal wage relativities of an enterprise. They are not, in the normal course of events,[7] *expected* to result in significant changes to wage relativities. In many respects, job evaluation systems are 'policy-capturing': they systematise what is already there, smoothing out the odd anomaly and providing a hierarchy of 'worth' within which new or changed jobs can be placed.

There are many pressures on evaluators to come up with 'expected' results, results which by and large reflect existing relativities, recognised by reference to the 'fiddle factor' in the job evaluation literature. This phrase refers to the adjustment of a score on one factor to bring a job into acceptable alignment with other jobs (Fonda et al., 1979:35).[8] In other words, the process of job evaluation, based as it is on the 'capturing' of organisational values as expressed through existing wage hierarchies, is not a technical process that exists in a vacuum, immune from the politics of organisational life (see Evans and Nelson, 1988). The industrial and economic implications of radical alteration to existing wage hierarchies influence the deliberations of evaluation committee members.

DO ANY JOB EVALUATION PRACTICES CONSTITUTE UNLAWFUL DISCRIMINATION?

Where job evaluation is used for pay-setting, a non-discriminatory system would lead to a situation where jobs of equal 'size' as measured by the scheme receive equal treatment under a pay-setting system regardless of the sex of the occupants.[9] Where under a job evaluation scheme a female-dominated classification is awarded the same points as a male-dominated one, then one would expect it to be slotted into the same grade for pay-setting purposes. If this is not the case, then under the *Sex Discrimination Act*, unlawful discrimination could be said to occur.

It would also appear that, under the *Sex Discrimination Act* which deals with indirect as well as direct discrimination, it would be possible for employees to bring complaints to the relevant agencies if they believed that the design of a scheme indirectly discriminated against people in female-dominated occupations or classifications, and/or that the implementation of the scheme directly or indirectly discriminated against people in female-dominated occupations or classifications. Even if the design of the scheme allows for the adequate acknowledgment of all the features of women's jobs, the implementation process may not. If in the evaluation of positions the demands of jobs predominantly filled by women gain less recognition than the demands of jobs predominantly held by men, then the administration of the scheme is discriminatory.

A job evaluation scheme is viewed as a neutral tool serving central organisational purposes. The application of neutral rules which have a disparate impact on men and women unrelated to work requirements or performance is indirectly discriminatory. This might be a problem in the process of collecting information about jobs. For example,

> there are skill, responsibility, stress and working condition characteristics prevalent in female-dominated jobs that rarely show up in job descriptions. If an employee is not asked about specific job

content or is asked incorrectly, she/he cannot respond. If there is no response, wages for that job will be less because it was not considered in the subsequent evaluation. (Steinberg and Haignere, 1985:14−14).

All these matters have received more attention in countries where equal pay for work of equal value legislation exists in one form or another. In Australia the *Sex Discrimination Act* has yet to be tested on these issues.

Little effort has been put into dealing with gender bias in job evaluation systems in Australia. Neither management consulting firms nor the management of organisations using job evaluation schemes have had any particular reason, before the development of affirmative action programs, to address the issue. It would appear, from the experience in other countries, that legislative pressure is a significant factor in the development of interest in the elimination of gender bias from the job evaluation process.

Many organisations in Australia use points-rating systems which, in the definition and weighting of factors, might contain a bias against the jobs held predominantly by women. This bias might then be exacerbated through implementation processes. People unfamiliar with the demands of women's jobs might make uninformed decisions about the levels of skill, effort and responsibility required to perform effectively in them. Furthermore, the current undervaluing of women's work is likely to be reinforced by the ways in which current relativities in pay and status inform the process, from the initial benchmark exercise (which 'captures' the organisation's values) through to the judgments made within evaluation committees.

Participation in the evaluation process by the various people whose jobs are affected, combined with adequate training of all those involved in how gender bias can enter position description writing and evaluation, might go some way towards reducing the possibility of gender bias.

Organisations which use formal job evaluation schemes would be expected, as part of their affirmative action programs, to have objects directed to this end.[10] These would include training and committee membership targets for female employees which might, in themselves, alter some traditional organisational values, given women's overall position in organisational hierarchies.

As organisations increasingly recognise the need to eliminate such bias, the consulting firms offering services in this field might become more responsive in their guidelines and consulting practices. Consulting firms will, one hopes, establish their own codes of practice directed to the elimination of gender bias, as have their counterparts in other countries.[11]

If organisations covered by the *Affirmative Action Act* are considering introducing job evaluation systems, the potential for gender bias in different systems and in implementation processes needs to be considered at the outset. There is scope, in the relationship set up with a consulting firm, to make clear the organisation's commitment to a system free of gender bias.

We need constantly to remind ourselves that what is being measured is a job's *relative* value, in relation to contributions to organisational objectives. This chapter has emphasised the subjectivity involved in the determination of the relative value of different kinds of work. There is much evidence to suggest that women's work is undervalued because it is performed by women, and because women, concentrated as they are at lower levels within work organisations, occupations and unions, have had little power to influence the relative value placed on their jobs.

These features of the overall situation do not allow us to be complacent about the results of current job evaluation exercises. We have to remind ourselves constantly that they are 'systematising subjective judgments. There is no "right answer", in the sense of an objectively correct evaluation' (Rubenstein, 1984:96) and the judgments are therefore open to review.

9 Moving towards pay equity using job evaluation

There is an increased interest in bringing formal job evaluation systems into various parts of the public sector; they are, of course, widely used in the private sector. The schemes being introduced — points-factor systems — have received much attention in the pay equity debate. In countries with pay equity legislation they are the preferred method to determine the relative value of female-dominated and male-dominated classifications.

Points-factor systems have been used extensively in the United States in comparable worth cases. Comparable worth is defined narrowly in the United States to distinguish it from the broader issue of pay equity which might include various strategies to raise the wages of women relative to men. In the United States comparable worth now means the use of a job evaluation scheme to compare the value of dissimilar work performed predominantly by men and women: the comparison of the value to the employer of jobs along dimensions of skill, effort, responsibility and working conditions in female-dominated and male-dominated occupations, for example the comparison of secretaries with truck drivers, or nurses with tree trimmers, or ambulance drivers with mental health nursing aides.

We have to understand the limited use that job evaluation has for pay equity results in the Australian context. One of the features of the early comparable worth claims in the United States was that points-factor evaluation was asked for by unions as a means of establishing the relative value of the female-dominated classifications which they believed were underpaid. A scheme was brought in specifically to provide evidence of current pay inequities. That occurred in a different industrial climate than that which is encouraging the use of job evaluation systems as part of award restructuring in Australia today. We cannot expect the application of a job evaluation system significantly to alter internal wage hierarchies, or more particularly the relative value of female-dominated classifications, if the pressure is not there to do so, if the pay equity issue is not an explicit concern of the process (see ch. 8).

Nevertheless, this is no reason why the attempt should not be made to apply the systems in such a way that the bias in them, dealt with in the previous chapter, is reduced. The rest of this chapter concentrates on what needs to be considered when introducing a job evaluation system to an organisation.

There is a lot of preparation required by management and employee associations before a scheme is introduced. The ideal starting point is the establishment of a steering committee to oversee the process, but the issue of representation on it immediately arises. The culture of the organisation might not be receptive to the broad representation that is probably needed for fair results. Yet job evaluation practitioners point to the importance of consensus and the acceptability of the system if it is going to work well. Representation on the steering committee is important in signalling from the outset whether consensus is to be broad-based or restricted to that which can be achieved from within a narrow range of participants.

The early decisions that need to be made by the steering committee include the coverage of the job evaluation system: what categories of employees would be covered initially, what categories might the scheme be extended to or not cover at all, what are the implications of covering different categories of employees by different schemes?

One needs to deal carefully with the situation where more than one system of job evaluation is used. Commonly, wages staff, management staff and non-management clerical staff are covered by different systems. In the case of wages staff and clerical staff, there are pay equity issues involved. For example, one might have a receptionist in a clerical structure and a receptionist on the wages side, one perhaps called a messenger or commissionaire position. Some of the functions of the job are the same, others are different. Some of the functions might be the same but are *perceived* differently, because the broader context of the job colours the perception of one part: are they both performing a security function, or is the male receptionist seen to be doing that and the female not? The female might be involved in telephone, mail, typing duties; the male is probably not. Yet the wages position is not covered by the same scheme as the clerical position. Should it be included, for relativity purposes, in the benchmark? What would the union's position be on this?

Next, the steering committee needs to choose systems with which to work, and there are various criteria which need to be used to guide the choice. For example, a scheme needs to be acceptable and credible for the range of positions it is to cover. It needs to be relatively easy to understand and work with. The organisation would have to decide on the advantages and disadvantages of using an 'off-the-shelf' system from a large firm which might be less flexible in certain respects than one from a smaller firm where the consultants own the system and might be more receptive to negotiations about modifications to the system. Alternatively, the organisations might wish to pursue the possibility of developing an in-house system, or substantially modifying an 'off-the-shelf' system to suit its own needs and purposes.

There is enormous flexibility in the way the evaluation process is carried out. It depends very much on the time and funding commitment the organisation is prepared to make, in consultants' fees and in the length of time it is prepared to put into the process; it also depends on the organisation's willingness to negotiate with the consultants on particular variations of the 'standard' approach.

The steering committee needs to establish what issues it would like to negotiate over in preliminary discussion with the consulting firms.

There might be a need in initial discussion with the consulting firms to clarify the factors that are measured, the weightings that are given to the factors and discover whether there is any modification possible in the factors that are used, in their weightings or in the interpretation of what the factors mean in practice.

Most, if not all, of the conventional schemes will need modification. For example, most schemes reflect traditional hierarchical organisational structures and collect information about supervisory work but not about teamwork situations, where close working relationships are based on coordination and close liaison.

Any factors and sub-factors that are being measured for job worth have to incorporate all the important and relevant differentiating characteristics of all jobs to which the scheme is going to be applied. It is likely that the schemes on offer have developed and were refined in contexts where attention was not drawn to the demands of female-dominated job categories and will therefore require modification. For example, clerk-typist positions and general office positions are not dealt with satisfactorily under most job evaluation schemes. Some of the demands of the positions are not tapped in the data-capturing instruments and are not then evaluated as components of the positions. There appears to be insufficient differentiation at the lower end of the task range, leading to the neglect of the range of complexity in jobs requiring filing, the different reading and writing language demands of different positions, the issue of the breadth of tasks performed and the different degrees of human relations skills involved in clerical positions (see also chapter 8).

It also appears that consistency in ratings is less likely in the evaluation of secretarial, steno-secretarial and clerk-typist jobs where specific tasks and skills involved are not well understood or are less readily identifiable and have not been built into the factors and sub-factors used in job evaluation systems. The same appears to be the case with service-oriented positions and policy advisory positions in the public sector.

Modifications have been made to the Hay system in the United States, particularly as far as the Human Relations and Accountability scores are concerned. As well, organisations have developed their own systems to account more adequately for the 'values' held, and which alter the usual Human Relations and Accountability measures.

For example, the idea of three levels of a Human Relations score seems easily contested. Some job categories cause problems here. Let's say that level 1 is normal courtesy, level 2 is influencing be-haviour, selling, and level 3 is changing the long-term behaviour of others. It may be that the work of telephonists (for example. in the classified ads section of the Melbourne *Age* (Reed, 1986) is not seen to be selling work, yet the women attract and retain clients and make a significant contribution to the sale of advertisement space. The qualities they have and apply are the ones salespeople are rewarded for. In customer service positions, many 'mature', experienced women are employed for the qualities they have developed in and out of the workforce, and are valued by the organisation because of the importance of these qualities in attracting and retaining customers. Is this level 1 or 2 on a Human Relations score? Here the organisation's culture and the use made of these people's skills might differ, as might the recognition of their use. It would be up to the organisation to determine, through the benchmark exercise, the value of this work relative to other positions and functions, and negotiate with the consulting firm about this relative value and its recognition through the system's use.

In the United States, the Hay system has sometimes been modified to take into account four levels of Human Relations skills, mindful of the particular types of public contact work carried out by public sector organisations, as against the private sector context within which the three Hay levels (basic, important, critical) were developed. (It could be said that with a deregulated banking and finance in-dustry and the recognition of the competitive edge customer service gives, even in the private sector this three-level classification is in-adequate. It could also be said that in the private sector it fails to recognise the Human Relations skills used in other predominantly female jobs.) The Oregon public service modified Hay because it was felt that the 'basic' level did not distinguish jobs with no public contact from those that required the courtesy and other skills which are applied when dealing with some members of the public. The final guidecharts have a four-level Human Relations skill sub-factor: incidental, basic, important and critical (SEIU, 1985).

In the Sacramento School District the Human Relations skills are incorporated into the Responsibility factor, which includes impact of the job on students and the public. Within these two sub-factors, there are four levels:

- ordinary courtesy in personal contact or contact by phone, involving an exchange of information; explaining policies, advising;

- some responsibility for influencing, counselling, and motivating others, resolving conflicts;

- considerable responsibility for these (SEIU, 1985).

The working conditions factor, rarely used by Hay for white-collar jobs (although increasingly being recognised in systems in the US and the UK) has been developed to recognise a variety of environments and features of work. Save the Children Fund (SCF) in the UK calls one factor Special Conditions. This includes mental stress (caused by such conditions as working in isolation or the monotony of repetitive work), physical environment and social factors (such as unsocial hours or 'providing services for particularly stigmatised groups'). Physical activity was measured as a separate factor, and included that involved in the occupation of childcare workers (EOR, 1988a). In Michigan, mental and visual strain is included; in the Sacramento School District plan, working conditions include the environment, and physical demands and hazards. In Oregon, where Hay was modified, there is a psychological work demand factor which measures the extent to which the job requires work under inflexible time guidelines, multiple roles or dealing with emotionally distressed people (SEIU, 1985).

As far as Responsibility was concerned, the SCF wanted to recognise the intangible assets of the organisation, namely its prestige and reputation. The effect of errors on the part of the job holder is recognised alongside responsibility for financial resources, staff and equipment (EOR, 1988a).

Another issue for negotiation revolves around the different ways in which job data can be collected, for the benchmark sample and for the rest of the jobs in the organisation. The organisation can invest a lot of resources in training job analysts to interview each job occupant and to observe them at work, and to write up a standard and comprehensive job description. Alternatively, analysts can be trained and then in large groups job occupants can fill in a questionnaire about their jobs, using analysts as a resource. The completed questionnaire can then be used as the job description evaluated by the evaluation committee, rather than the detailed, narrative job description being used; alternatively, both sets of data might be made available to the evaluation committee.

Also for negotiation are the additional training requirements that an organisation would require if the scheme's introduction were to be consistent with the organisation's equal employment opportunity program. These would include the training of job analysts, job evaluators and job occupants and anyone involved in the process in relation to the points at which gender and race bias might come into the system.

There needs to be a commitment to training and educating people further down the organisational hierarchy about the process of evaluation. Before its abolition, the NSW Public Service Board, in preparation for the introduction of a new Clerical Officer classification, ran job analysis workshops for secretarial and keyboard staff, designed to draw out from job occupants the various skills used in the activities with which they had been involved in their jobs, so that they gained a better sense of the value of the work they performed (Mary McLeod, pers. comm.). Similarly, before answering a questionnaire about the nature of their jobs, secretarial staff at Kuring-gai College of Advanced Education were given a briefing paper which alerted them to the ways in which they might, in their answers, contribute to an under-valuation of their work. They took the opportunity, too, to discuss the questionnaire among themselves. These are important mechanisms to employ if the objective is to have people participating equally and effectively in the evaluation process.

Part of the initial negotiation should be about representation on job evaluation and related committees. For example, what gender balance will there be? The SCF in the UK determined that there would be representation of men and women on the steering committee and on the evaluation committees. Indeed, the evaluation committee was balanced to reflect the interests of men and women, management and non-management and black and white people. The advisory committee set up to monitor the scheme and deal with appeals also had a gender balance (EOR, 1988a).

Consensus is the basis for the determination of the value base and the relative ranking of the benchmark positions, and, later, for the evaluation of jobs. Consensus, though, can be arrived at in different ways, and it might be more apparent than real. To illustrate: the organisation might be aware that there are widely differing views on the value of secretarial and keyboard work. The management consultant emphasises the importance of selecting people for evaluation committees who will make constructive contributions, who will not be challenging the overall job evaluation process and who will be assertive but not disruptive. They may feel that existing secretarial and keyboard staff at lower levels will be intimidated by the process and will therefore not make a valuable, independent contribution. Some of these staff might be known to be actively working for a greater recognition of the value of their work and might be seen to be lacking 'objectivity'. Safe representation of these workers might be seen to be a private secretary who has gone through the secretarial/keyboard ranks, or a clerical worker who used to be in secretarial/keyboard ranks, or a supervisor of keyboard workers. We found that to be a problem in the membership of evaluation committees at the South Australian College of Advanced Education (Burton et al., 1987). The people so chosen are likely to reflect management's (sometimes genuinely uninformed) views of the relative value of this work, for the range of reasons we explored in *Women's Worth*.

What about the role of the EEO coordinator? While race and sex bias in the job evaluation process is little understood, there is a continuing role for this officer. The EEO coordinator should be an observer at meetings, or as many as s/he can afford to attend, to report on the process from an EEO point of view. S/he should have access to all the consultation processes and the decisions and be given the opportunity to be trained as an evaluator and job analyst, so that s/he is able to act as a resource for staff when necessary. But all this should occur in conjunction with processes to ensure the integration of EEO principles into the exercise. The selection of committee members should be on EEO-related criteria.

It is usually the case that a manager from Personnel, Industrial Relations or the Human Resources Management area is chosen to chair the evaluation committee meetings. But the influence of that person's ideas on the evaluation committee members can be very strong and can affect the ranking outcomes. The chairperson should be a facilitator and it would be appropriate to rotate the position to minimise the risk of undue influence of particular people.

Another issue to raise with consultants at the outset relates to information disclosure. What information about the process will be disclosed to whom? Most consultant firms argue that the points rating given to particular jobs should not be generally known. The relationship between points and salary ranges for different job categories may or may not be generally disclosed. Yet in some instances the decision has been made to publish raw points and to allow an appeal process on the results (e.g. SEIU, 1985).

The consulting firm should be one which is aware of the EEO issues in system design and implementation. Consultants (even individuals within the one firm) vary. If EEO or pay equity guidelines have been developed by the firm — for example those put out by Hay in Britain (Fouracre, 1984) and Canada — they should be used. The consultants should be asked if they have developed their own guidelines. (See Equal Opportunities Commission, 1985b; Fonda et al., 1979; Burton et al., 1987.)

Once a system is chosen and coverage is determined there needs to be a flow chart of events widely accessible so people know what is going on, so that involvement can be organised and employees and their representatives are informed about the total process. Certain types of briefing sessions need to begin, keeping people informed generally. If the consulting firm has not used EEO guidelines in the past or has not developed an EEO code of practice, then briefing on sex and race bias needs to occur for the consultants themselves.

The organisation needs to deal explicitly and deliberately with the question of how the organisational culture is to be conveyed to the consulting firm. In initial meetings, an important component of the interaction between the consultants and the organisation is the conveying of the organisation's values and mission to the consultants who need an understanding of the organisation's past, its traditions, recent changes in corporate philosophy, the reasons for things being as they are and the reasons the organisation might have for moving to the use of a formal job evaluation system.

The organisational culture is understood by the consultants from what they are told, from their own observations and from the documentation to which they will seek to have access. They spend more time with personnel and other managers than they do with non-management staff, keyboard workers, technical and professional staff, clerical workers and other employees. They are likely to give weight to the views of the managers they are interacting with as being more knowledgeable and less partisan organisational participants. It is at this point that they will establish whether pay equity is on the organisation's agenda.

It would be useful if the consultants were made aware of any lack of consensus on the relative value of particular job categories which might have been aired within the organisation from time to time and they should have access to the different points of view. Then the consultants have an obligation to look closely at the job categories in question. It may be, for example, that a particular category of female-dominated jobs has been a matter for dispute in the past. The management of the organisation is not necessarily well informed about the issues involved in an adequate assessment of the demands of those jobs in work value terms.

To illustrate: the practice of employing 'mature' women with previous work experience and with childcare responsibilities behind them reduces the time required to train them in some positions. Yet the training time required for effective performance is one thing which is measured and attracts value under a job evaluation scheme. The organisation recognises the skills — particularly Human Relations, but also capacity to work under pressure, product and industry knowledge, speed and accuracy — that are drawn on but they do not necessarily get acknowledged through the job evaluation process. Is the time the women spend in home management counted in lieu of training time? The SCF scheme, under its factor Essential Skills, includes 'life experiences' gained either in the home or social environment, such as childcare skills or work with community organisations (EOR, 1988a).

The consultant might be aware of the use the organisation makes of people's community experiences, and respond to management's use of the word 'mature' with a comment along those lines, but will give the organisation some leeway to determine the value of the positions according to their 'culture'. Here culture includes traditional internal relativities in pay and, unfortunately, the acknowledged but unrewarded use of women's skills (often referred to as natural or feminine abilities). It is not the consultant who determines the final outcome, although s/he might point out certain features or advise in a certain direction. The consulting firm is careful to work with the value system of the client organisation rather than imposing another set of values. The responsibility for altering traditional understandings is with the client organisation, and provides additional reason for broad representation on the steering committee.

10 Gender bias in the performance assessment process

This chapter details the results of research I conducted into the performance appraisal process within a large Australian finance company (which I call here INSOLV). In the analysis of the data I collected, I did not attempt to quantify any results. I wished, rather, to pursue through conversation and discussion what people's perceptions and experiences were, and to discover whether comments made on performance appraisal forms reflected discriminatory attitudes towards women.

This means that the research finds are suggestive rather than conclusive, and could themselves guide decisions within the company on what data might be usefully collected, and what strategies might be implemented to reduce the possibility of gender bias in the performance appraisal and other processes.

I interviewed eight men and six women for between an hour and an hour and a half. I had a list of areas that I wanted to touch on during the interview and I took notes as we spoke. I covered three broad areas: the interviewees' experiences of the performance appraisal process, their assessment of its overall effectiveness, and their perception of the position of women within the company.

The positions the interviewees held were:

Branch manager	(male)
Manager, sub-branch	(male)
Sales representative	(male)
Credit manager	(male)
Sales manager	(male)
New business manager	(male)
Customer finance officer	(male)
2 new business officers	(1 male, 1 female)
Accounts supervisor	(female)

General hand clerical officer (female)
Switchboard operator   (female)
Cashier   (female)

In addition, I had copies of performance appraisal forms extending back two to four years, for 90 females and 85 males, covering the range of positions allocated from 180 to 550 Hay points. I had a research assistant helping me go through the forms, looking at comments made by interviewees and raters and relating these to the recommendations for promotion and development opportunities, and comparing the performance appraisals of men and women.

It is difficult to talk about the performance appraisal process in isolation from other employment practices, some of which feed into the ways in which women are dealt with when being appraised.

Although an increasing number of women are being employed as classified officers, it is striking nevertheless to observe the all-female clerical ranks. Many interviewees commented on this practice and the fact that it was not based on any objective assessment of people's capabilities or interests. Several people said that when women made inquiries about classified officer positions, such as customer services officer, they would be discouraged from applying, on the grounds that they would find the job too difficult. Some said that a picture of the job was presented to women which did not reflect the reality of it. For example, women would be given the impression that it involved 'knocking on people's doors and trying to get money out of them', whereas in fact the contact with customers was mainly by phone, and visits to people's homes, when they occurred, would mostly be done by two people. (One interviewee said that he thought a man and a woman together in this situation would probably be more effective than two men.)

Many women enter, then, as clerical staff. They can continue as clerical officers for a considerable time, moving from one type of job to another, gathering experience and, in some instances, becoming more interested in assuming a classified officer position.

But there is no clear-cut career progression either within the clerical ranks or from clerical to classified officer ranks, and some people expressed the view that this leads to the recruitment of 'the wrong sort of person'. What is meant by this is that the company offers little in the way of salary and career rewards for clerical officers, so that it is more likely to attract people who do not have aspirations for career progression. This is, in fact, only partly true.

It may suit the company to operate in this way, but there is no doubt that this practice is to the detriment of many women who are interested in career progression and more interesting work.

I was told that competent women don't stay in the company,

because it does not offer career prospects for them. I was also told that some clerical officers are staying long enough to become classified officers, so that their chances of finding a career position in another company within the finance industry are enhanced. In other words, it would not be in their long-term interests to move while they are still clerical officers, so their decision to deal with what they regard as inequitable conditions by staying with the company is precisely to give them a greater chance for opportunities elsewhere.

There was widespread agreement that women in clerical ranks who finally moved to classified officer positions 'took too long', that they were only reluctantly given the chance, and usually after having performed some of the duties of classified officer positions for some time.

In other words, and many people commented along these lines, women had to prove themselves over a considerable period, and this usually meant having eventually to 'spit out their dummy' (a phrase I heard several times) to indicate to management that they were serious about their desire to become classified officers. This was recognised to be risky. It might mean that a woman was then given a chance, but it could equally mean a negative performance appraisal, as far as the person's attitude was concerned.

This has a direct consequence for the way in which the performance appraisal process operates for women and men. There is a form of indirect discrimination operating as far as women are concerned. It works in the following way.

I asked several people what they thought 'adaptability' on the appraisal form meant. Generally speaking, a central component of 'adaptability' was the ability and willingness of staff to take on work outside their own area, to help out others when they were overloaded with work, to accept supervisors' requests to drop what they were doing and take on something else. Consider the different situations for a female clerical officer and a male classified officer. One supervisor I interviewed said that clerical officers would be appraised on accuracy and speed in carrying out their work, and on their 'making time to help other people' complete their work. The clerical officer can see no tangible reward, has no means of having the extra work acknowledged in terms of remuneration, and may be asked to help out on work usually performed by a classified officer who receives an income considerably higher than hers.

It is not because she is a woman that she might resent being asked to help out in this way. It is because she has made a realistic assessment of the relationship between the work demanded of her and the rewards she might expect from doing it. The male officer, on the other hand, knows that to be flexible in this way will be looked upon favourably in his performance appraisal. There are tangible rewards to look forward to if he demonstrates adaptability in this way.

Resentment was expressed by female clerical officers for the inequities of a situation where they were expected to be 'adaptable' while there was no expectation that it would make their prospects for gaining a classified officer position any more likely. This is combined with a situation where, although they have expressed interest in such a move, and they have accumulated years of service, they observe young men coming in from outside the office into classified officer vacancies. For some female clerical officers, this means they are helping to train young men in the work involved on their route to becoming classified officers.

Experts in performance appraisal systems (see for example Richards, 1984:82; Lansbury, 1981:12−13; Kane and Lawler, 1979:445) recommend that characteristics such as 'adaptability', 'dependability' and 'attitude' should not be included as elements to be appraised, because of the high degree of subjectivity in their assessment. It is believed that work-related behaviour, rather than attitudes or personality characteristics, should be assessed. Few of the men I interviewed felt that there were any problems with the measurement of these characteristics, and this is not surprising. They benefited, in career terms, if they could demonstrate their adaptability, dependability, and their positive attitudes. But they are, structurally speaking, in a different situation from the women as far as the assessment of these characteristics is concerned.

I have already indicated how their situations differ, but another example might be helpful. A young male new business officer was favourably appraised for his attitude, in that he 'accepts company policy without question'. It would be hard for a career-minded female clerical officer to accept company policy without question, because if she did she would not progress very far. Yet when she questions it she is likely to receive an unfavourable assessment in relation to her attitude. One woman received a 1 on attitude on her first appraisal, she believed because she 'speaks her mind'. Another received a 2 and there was a reference to her 'temper'; she attributes that to her response when asked to do the work of another officer as well as her own work, when she felt that this was not going to be acknowledged in any tangible way.

Many people, men and women, expressed some disquiet about the demands made of female clerical officers when considered in relation to their relatively low pay and lack of encouragement in relation to career progression. There was widespread belief that, for those who did eventually gain classified officer status, it came far too late, and, for a time, the woman in question was likely to be paid less than other classified officers and to continue to perform some clerical duties as well as her new duties. This seems to be a way of 'testing' whether she really is serious in her career intentions, as well, of course, as being a cost-saving measure.

Given the recruitment practice of employing women for clerical positions, and men (and some women) for classified officer positions, combined with a widespread reluctance to promote women from clerical to classified officer positions, regardless of their demonstrated ability and interest, it is considerably harder for women to make careers within the finance industry (or at least within this finance company) than it is for men. While this is the case, the company is unlikely to attract as many career-minded women as are available in the community.

A case study is appended to this chapter which demonstrates some potential outcomes of the practices of the company. In the case study I have drawn particular attention to the 'mobility rule' and its interpretation in practice. Although it is not formal policy of the company to require mobility, everyone agreed, and their views were supported by comments made on performance appraisal forms, that lack of mobility affected promotional opportunities. The rule is interpreted in practice in such a way that women's career progression is affected much more than men's. (The case study is written as if it describes the situation in an insurance company, to avoid any possibility of identification of the actual company used.)

As with most organisational rules, this one can be interpreted flexibly, depending on the priorities and values of the decision-makers. It appeared that women who indicated they were not mobile around the State were not considered for promotion. This is quite clear in the comments made on many performance appraisal forms. Yet it is not so clear that this is an inflexible rule as far as men are concerned. There appears to be more sensitivity to difficult or unusual family circumstances for men than for women, so that a man's promotion might be put 'on hold', given these circumstances, while a woman's would be unlikely to be considered again. For example, one man received the following comment: 'X has expressed the desire to remain at — for a while. This I believe is due to personal problems rather than a lack of ambition. Given proper support at this stage of his employment I think that he could develop into a very worthwhile executive.'

It was made clear to me that men would say that they were mobile, even if they had made up their minds that they were unlikely to accept a move. They were aware of the importance of indicating their willingness to move. Women were more likely to be straightforward about their situation, and say if they were indeed not mobile.

Single, mobile women are less likely to be asked about their future plans than young men. Regardless of what they express for themselves in career terms, they are perceived as a risk. So are married women. I was told by one manager that 'married women are as difficult as single women, because their husbands might be asked to transfer'. The young, mobile, career-oriented women see their male peers move into junior management while they are trying to move into classified officer positions. An older, married woman, whose family responsibilities are nearly over, and who has enough experience of various positions in the company that she would like to build on in a classified officer's position, sees no possibility of it happening, despite the support she receives from her immediate supervisor. Her view is supported by a comment on an appraisal form, 'at 45 years of age she [a customer services officer] is not being considered for promotion prospects'.

There appear to be quite different levels of encouragement given to male and female officers. One woman interested in becoming a customer finance officer (CFO) was told that the training for the position was on the job. It was only later that she discovered that three of her male colleagues were being trained at State Office for such a position. Another woman was being trained by a CFO alongside a State trainee, without previous finance background, and his salary during the period was considerably more than hers.

Women who have gained lengthy on-the-job experience, who are expected to use it, often beyond their own position duties, who are on a lot less money than their male counterparts, and who aspire to become classified officers, watch young, inexperienced men gain opportunities and get ahead on higher incomes than themselves. Their feelings are bound to be expressed in attitudes which receive negative comments at the time of performance appraisal. Yet they have sound reasons for feeling the way they do.

It appears that there are some young male managers who share the women's disquiet about the general situation of women employees within the company, and do their best to encourage them and to promote their opportunities. Yet they are not in a position to have a final say. This was clear to me through interviews and through comments on appraisal forms by immediate supervisors and reviewing officers. An immediate supervisor recommending promotion of a woman from clerical to classified officer ranks is not necessarily going to get the support of a reviewing officer. The scepticism about a woman's capacity, or interest, or long-term availability, is there and informs decisions about whether she will be offered an opportunity to progress.

For many of these women, it appears that their lengthy experience in a range of clerical and classified officer positions is taken advantage of by the company without this being acknowledged through remuneration or advancement. Frequently on appraisal forms there was a comment on these people along the lines of 'X is more than happy to be left in the position of CFO as she is happy doing the work'; 'well suited to her current role and it will suit us to have her there for a longer period'; 'It suits us to have her in this role'. Frequently the statement that the woman being appraised is 'not promotable' (regardless of the level of competence she is judged to have in the position) is not supported by any good reason.

There appears to be considerable pressure on women to accept that they should not fill a position identified as useful for developmental purposes to career officers. This was a view expressed to me in interviews, and is supported by comments on performance appraisal forms. For a woman who said, on her appraisal form, 'I would enjoy the challenge of an executive position should the opportunity arise', the reviewer commented that 'X has acknowledged that if a promotion came her way, she would have to "stand aside" and accept a possible demotion if it was the company's desire to train someone else in that position'. For another, a female new business manager who was not mobile, 'X will not be placed in a position where she will prevent a person who wishes to get ahead gaining experience in that position'.

It would appear that the same behaviours might well be interpreted differently, depending on whether the person being appraised was a male or a female (something we commented on extensively in *Women's Worth*). It is hard to be certain about interpreting some of the following comments, but they are worthy of further investigation, given the evidence of 'sex-congruent' responses to people's attitudes and behaviour. For a female customer service manager, the following comment, 'X acts on impulse at times as a result of her keenness to achieve better results', can be compared with the comment for a male officer, 'X accepts the need for calculated risk taking'.

Men's 'aggressive' behaviour is commented upon favourably. One man received the following comment in the overall assessment of his performance: 'X's aggressive attitude towards his career is the main driving force to become successful which can result in high expectations.' The evaluating executives say of him, despite competent, rather than commendable ratings, 'X tends to want his career aspirations realised overnight. He will develop into a worthwhile executive'. X says of himself, 'I aspire to become a senior executive in the comming [sic] years'.

There is a great deal of research evidence to suggest that men's good performance is more likely to be attributed to ability, and women's to effort, and this affects promotional opportunities, as ability is more likely to be rewarded. It is difficult to judge, from the performance appraisal forms, whether this is a factor in the apparently slower rate of advancement of women than of men, but it might be a contributing factor. The following comments illustrate the point. A female was referred to as 'an operator who is capable of producing very good results *through determination and effort*'; '*her experience* means she has ability in this area'; 'with officer's *experience*, constantly showing excellent ability in this area'. A female executive with commendable ratings receives these comments: 'puts in the *effort* to gather facts and makes good recommendations'; 'put in additional *effort* and handled staff shortages . . . very well'; 'putting in additional *effort* and achieving good results'.

Male officers appear to receive more straightforward assessments of their ability, which is not as readily attributed to experience: 'has *ability* to gather and evaluate facts'; 'has an *inbuilt ability* to comprehend and evaluate accurately written and oral material'. A man who was later demoted from a credit supervisor position to an officer position was nevertheless seen as having 'a lot of *potential*' in the area of supervisory leadership, 'a lot of *potential* yet to be developed' in the area of employee development, and '*potential* which will be developed with further experience' in decision-making. Potential, it sometimes appears, is something men are assumed to have (until it becomes clear, usually after a promotion, that they have not) and women have to prove that they have.

Reflected in some of the comments are perceptions of company policy, whether formal or informal. For example, for a woman who was a sales representative and is now a new business manager, 'naturally sales manager role would depend on company attitudes, nevertheless X does display the necessary attributes'. On the appraisal forms of another female officer who received a commendable rating while in a dealer finance officer position, the officer expressed an interest in moving to a sales position, which, in the evaluators' opinion, she could handle. The reviewer's comment, though, was 'whilst X is an excellent credit officer, particularly in dealer finance, it is considered that she is at this stage more suited to a credit roll [*sic*]'.

I gained the impression from reading many performance appraisal forms that men were more often given the benefit of any doubt there might be about their competence, whereas women would have to wait longer and prove themselves beyond any doubt before they received acknowlegment of their capacity to advance. The comments of some of the female officers indicate their frustration. For example, a female new business officer with commendable ratings each year was moved to say, 'I feel that the above assessment is good, however, this is the third assessment I've had with competent or better and I feel management hasn't seen my potential'. The following year, as a customer finance officer, she says of her commendable rating, 'I feel this review gives a fair assessment as that in past few months I have

121

had indications that a good result such as this will pay dividends to my career in the near future'. In the next year, still as a CFO, she says, 'Hopefully consistent performance in all areas will be noted'.

A female credit officer, in 1984, when she received a commendable rating, expressed the view that 'as I mainly work unsupervised and have been working happily with INSOLV I feel ... if I were male I would now be a credit executive'. Her promotion prospects were recorded as being for a credit executive position and that she was ready for such a position immediately. In the following year, still as a credit officer, and again with a commendable rating, she was deemed ready for a credit executive position in one year's time.

On the whole, the people I interviewed were very vague about the company's affirmative action program. Many were not aware of the existence of the *Sex Discrimination Act* or of the *Affirmative Action (Equal Employment Opportunity for Women) Act* and were certainly not informed about their rights under such legislation. Some commented on the circumstances under which they filled out a questionnaire, apparently designed to gather information for the affirmative action program. They worried about lack of anonymity and about the purposes to which the information might be put. It was quite clear to me that adequate communication and expressions of commitment to the program had not been forthcoming from management. This would appear to be a problem not just at the branch level but at higher levels where the program is developed and coordinated.

CASE STUDY

Marcus and Jane, Maria and Don all enter a private sector company in the finance, banking and insurance industry on the same day, all at between the ages of 18 and 21. On the recruitment form they are asked whether they are mobile within the State for transfer and promotional purposes. Marcus, Don and Maria answer that they are, Jane that she is not. Marcus was advised by his contacts in the organisation to answer in this way, even though he is deeply committed to caring for his mother who is an invalid at home, and who has many reasons for staying in her familiar environment. He was assured by his acquaintances in the firm that he would not be forced to move. Don had no trouble answering in this way. In a few years' time, when he has children, he would respond differently, because he would like to give them a stable home and school environment. But at the present time he would be prepared to move for a promotional opportunity. Maria, a single woman whose parents have work histories in the industry, aspires to be a top salesperson as a route to

higher positions, and has no difficulty answering the question. Whatever household arrangements she might make she is deeply committed to a career in the industry. Jane, reluctantly, because she too
wants a career, recognises that she would be hard put to move: she is
very close to her family and they rely on her for social and emotional
support.

After eight years with the same employers, Marcus and Don are
managers of branches in the metropolitan area, Don having spent six
months in a branch on the central coast, Marcus having moved
across three locations within the metropolitan region. Maria has
moved from clerical work into a classified officer position and Jane
has left, having spent four years in a clerical position and one year as
a classified officer selling insurance. She has joined another company
which has a policy of encouraging women into sales work on the
grounds that women do it better.

The question about mobility on the recruitment form is a screening
device. It is saying, in effect, 'how committed are you to the organisation and to a career? If the answer is yes and you are a male, then
there are very flexible ways in which the rule might apply, and
anyway, the organisation does not actually need everyone to be
mobile. So there is no real problem, in fact many managers have
never had to relocate.'

The formal policy of the organisation is not that mobility is a
prerequisite for promotions, but the posing of the question and the
selective use of the answers legitimates the informal policy which is
that flexible arrangements can be made for men but whatever women
answer, they are nevertheless treated as unlikely to be able to relocate.
On Jane's appraisal form each year, in answer to the question about
positions she is ready to be promoted into, the answer is 'nil: not
mobile'. On Maria's form the answer is vaguer and indicates that she
might be ready for several positions in one or two years' time. She
was, in fact, moved from position to position and branch to branch
in a relief capacity, and became very knowledgeable about the
company's activities and is therefore now an excellent officer, and is
likely to be promoted in the future. But she is progressing more
slowly than her male counterparts. Her form has vaguer answers
because the managers appraising her are worried about two things:
1) that she will marry and have children and not be mobile or,
indeed, will leave to have a family, thus wasting the training and
developmental opportunities given to her; and 2) that she will marry
and her husband will be asked to relocate by *his* company, thus again
wasting her training and opportunities.

When asked why women are not given the same opportunities as
men in the company, most—not all—male managers answer along
the above lines. When the female clerical officer staff are asked, they

say: women who want careers leave this company, they know the opportunities are not good. So we have a self-fulfilling prophecy operating here, with a particular result. Of the population of women entering this organisation, some want careers and do not get them; others, because of the constraints of husband and family, and not having been encouraged by organisational practices to believe that within those constraints there might be other possibilities, come to define themselves as wanting jobs not careers, reinforcing the view about women in general that the managers hold.

11 Equal opportunities and equal pay for work of equal value in Australia

In Australia the statutory framework through which equal pay for work of equal value may be implemented covers a broad area of Commonwealth and State industrial and anti-discrimination legislation. The regulation of the terms and conditions of employment has only recently become a matter relevant to both industrial tribunals and anti-discrimination bodies.[1] The relationship between industrial legislation concerned with wage-fixing through the process of industrial arbitration, and anti-discrimination legislation concerned with eliminating discrimination in employment, is yet to develop fully in the area of pay equity.

Industrial legislation

Equal pay for work of equal value has traditionally been determined in Australia in an industrial context (Women's Bureau, 1988a:11 DEIR, 1985:1). Claims for it have been regarded as industrial matters to be addressed by the appropriate Commonwealth or State industrial tribunal responsible for fixing minimum award wages.

While a complex range of industrial legislation exists to regulate wages through industrial arbitration,[2] on the whole there are no express statutory provisions[3] contained under Commonwealth legislation requiring the implementation of equal pay for work of equal value. The statutory provisions which exist under State law in relation to equal pay provide for the application of pay equity principles only in very limited circumstances. The concept of equal pay for work of equal value has not therefore been defined and applied as a result of legislated standards. Rather, it is a principle that has been adopted by

125

Commonwealth and State industrial tribunals in the course of industrial wage fixation.

This process has been significantly shaped through the operation of the former Australian Conciliation and Arbitration Commission (ACAC), which established the principle of equal pay for work of equal value in the 1972 *Equal Pay Case* (Equal Pay Decision Print B8506, 1972). The ACAC's adoption of the equal pay principle in 1972 provided for the implementation of equal pay for work of equal value with in awards made by agreement between parties to an industrial matter, or determined through the process of industrial arbitration. The principle has since been adopted by various State industrial tribunals.[4]

No precise definition of equal pay for work of equal value has been formulated by either the ACAC or the State bodies involved in the determination of equal pay claims. Access to bias-free job evaluation as required for example within the United Kingdom[5] and certain parts of Canada[6] has not been regarded as a necessary requirement for the implementation of equal pay for work of equal value.

In March 1989 the functions of the ACAC in relation to the conciliation and arbitration of industrial disputes were transferred to the Commonwealth Industrial Relations Commission under the terms of the *Industrial Relations Act* 1988. Section 93 of the Act provides that: 'In the performance of its functions, the Commission shall take account of the principles embodied in ... the *Sex Discrimination Act* 1984 relating to discrimination in relation to employment.' In addition the Commission is required under section 90 of the Act to have regard to the likely effects on the national economy of any awards or orders, with special reference to the level of employment and inflation.

While significant developments have occurred through the industrial arbitration system in relation to the application of the principle of equal pay for equal work, the achievements made in the area of equal pay for work of equal value have been ad hoc and limited to particular cases (Short, 1986:315). The extent to which the *Industrial Relations Act* will alter this situation is yet to be determined.

Anti-discrimination legislation

Discrimination in relation to employment is prohibited throughout Australia under Commonwealth and State law.[7] Under this legislation an employer may commit an act of unlawful discrimination if the payment of different wage rates involves either direct or indirect discrimination. The Commonwealth *Sex Discrimination Act* 1984, which operates in each State and Territory, prohibits direct and indirect discrimination on the grounds of sex in the terms and conditions of employment.

In interpreting these provisions reference to *Convention on the Elimination of All Forms of Discrimination Against Women* can be made. This Convention is scheduled in the *Sex Discrimination Act*, and provides through Article 11 1 d) for 'the right to equal remuneration, including benefits, and to equal treatment in respect of work of equal value, as well as equality of treatment in the evaluation of the quality of work'.

Under the provisions of Commonwealth and State anti-discrimination legislation, complaints of discrimination can be lodged with the anti-discrimination agencies where attempts will be made to settle the complaint through the process of conciliation. In the case of the Commonwealth *Sex Discrimination Act*, representative complaints may also be lodged by unions and women's representative groups. Where conciliation is unsuccessful, the complaint may then be referred to the relevant anti-discrimination tribunal for formal hearing.

Once the evidence concerning a complaint of unlawful discrimination has been heard by the tribunal, it can either dismiss the complaint or make any of the following determinations:

- a declaration that the employer has engaged in unlawful conduct and should not repeat such conduct;

- a declaration that the employer should perform any reasonable act to redress any damage suffered by the complainant;

- a declaration that the employer should pay damages;

- a declaration that it would be inappropriate for any further action to be taken.

Determinations made by State anti-discrimination tribunals are enforceable in the same way as a judgment debt is enforced in a court of law. Enforcement under the Commonwealth *Sex Discrimination Act* is carried out by application to the Federal Court.

Despite the availability of procedures for the review of alleged discrimination in the terms and conditions of employment, there have been no wage discrimination claims brought under the Commonwealth *Sex Discrimination Act* 1984. The use of anti-discrimination legislation in relation to pay equity matters has been limited to several isolated, and on the whole unsuccessful, cases arising under State law.[8]

Anti-discrimination legislation has had little impact therefore on the implementation of the principle of equal pay for work of equal value. The reasons for this relate in part to the exemptions provided under Commonwealth and certain State discrimination laws to employers acting in accordance with orders and awards of industrial wage fixing tribunals. These exemptions will now be briefly discussed.

Although anti-discrimination legislation contemplates the review of discriminatory terms or conditions of employment, the availability of legal remedies in relation to wage discrimination claims is limited under Commonwealth law, and under State law in Victoria and New South Wales by exemptions given to persons acting in direct compliance with orders or awards of courts and tribunals having the power to fix industrial award wages.[9] The effect of these exemptions is to limit the application of anti-discrimination legislation to wage reviews where no order or award of a wage-fixing tribunal applies. In Australia where approximately 85 per cent of wage rates are determined by industrial tribunals (O'Donnell and Hall, 1988:48), the extent to which anti-discrimination legislation can apply to equal pay claims against employers is therefore largely restricted.

While complaints of discrimination might be made where no award provision exists, or in the States of Western Australia and South Australia, where no statutory protection is provided[10] to persons acting in compliance with discriminatory awards, the outcome of any such claims is uncertain. There are difficulties in interpreting what constitutes 'discrimination' and in deciding the meaning of 'terms and conditions' of employment as defined by anti-discrimination legislation.

The exemptions provided to people acting in compliance with industrial orders or awards were apparently introduced to preserve the authority of industrial wage-fixing tribunals and protect employers from experiencing a dual liability when complying with the terms of an award which contravenes anti-discrimination law. These exemptions do not however, expressly extend to the actual making of orders or awards by industrial wage-fixing authorities.[11]

This distinction is particularly important in the area of equal pay when considering the provisions of the Commonwealth *Sex Discrimination Act* and its possible impact on the operation of the Commonwealth Industrial Relations Commission in determining awards, orders and national wage-fixing principles. Arguably any statutory exemption could not be interpreted as providing the means by which discrimination in the payment of wage rates can be authorised under cover of industrial award determinations or other orders.

The general scheme of the Commonwealth *Sex Discrimination Act*, more over, suggests that as of August 1984 all Commonwealth awards would be made in accordance with the Act's provisions. This accords with the general principle that no award or order of a federal industrial tribunal can be made inconsistently with Commonwealth law.[12] It is also consistent with section 86 of the *Industrial Relations*

(Consequential Provisions) Act 1988 by which the *Sex Discrimination Act* has been made a prescribed Act for the purposes of section 121 of the *Industrial Relations Act* 1988.

It should be emphasised that the legal relationship between the Industrial Relations Commission and the *Sex Discrimination Act* is at this stage unclear in so far as the implementation of equal pay for work of equal value is concerned. The extent to which the Commonwealth *Sex Discrimination Act* may affect the Commission in the exercise of its functions remains untested in the area of equal pay.

The difficulties encountered in the interpretation of legislation touching on pay equity issues was a matter recently addressed in the *OECD Report to the Working Party on the Role of Women in the Economy* (Women's Bureau, 1988a). The report was directed to examining the institutional and legislative background of equal pay for work of equal value. Its final conclusions referred to the need for 'clear legislation incorporating simple judicial mechanisms' (1988a:28). In Australia such developments are yet to take effect.

In order to develop effective policies to enable development towards equal pay for work of equal value a wide range of EEO measures needs to be considered. As well as legislation prohibiting discrimination in employment there is also a body of legislation relating to EEO which may assist in the implementation of equal pay for work of equal value (see chapter 7).

International treaty obligations

There are three international instruments which relate to equal pay for work of equal value and to which Australia is a signatory:

1 The *Convention on the Elimination of all Forms of Discrimination Against Women* (CEDAW);

2 ILO *Convention No. 100 Concerning Equal Remuneration for Men and Women Workers for Work of Equal Value*; and

3 ILO *Convention No. 111 Concerning Discrimination in Respect of Employment and Occupation.*

The constitutional validity of all Commonwealth anti-discrimination legislation is dependent on the ratification by the Australian Government of international treaties such as CEDAW in the exercise of the external affairs power under section 51 (xxix) of the Australian Constitution.

With the introduction of the *Sex Discrimination Act* in 1984, certain provisions of CEDAW became implemented within Australian domestic law. It would appear that these provisions included Article

11(1)(d) which provides for the right to equal treatment for work of equal value, as well as equality of treatment in the evaluation of work.

ILO Convention No. 111 has also been implemented into Australian domestic law through the provisions of the *Human Rights and Equal Opportunity Commission Act* 1986. Article 2 of this Convention requires that:

> Each member for which the Convention is in force undertakes to declare and pursue a national policy designed to promote by methods appropriate to national conditions and practice, equality of opportunity and treatment in respect of employment and occupation, with a view to eliminating any discrimination with respect thereof.

The provisions introduced with the *Human Rights and Equal Opportunity Commission Act* give the Human Rights and Equal Opportunity Commission limited powers to conciliate complaints about discrimination in employment, and to report any acts or practices inconsistent with the principles contained within the Convention to the Federal Attorney-General.[13]

ILO Convention No. 100 requires in Article 2 that:

> Each member shall by means appropriate to the methods in operation for determining rates of remuneration, promote and in so far as is consistent with such methods, ensure the application to all workers of the principle of equal remuneration for men and women workers for work of equal value.

The obligations arising under the various international treaties concerning pay equity cover a wide range of measures including legislative, statutory and administrative reform as well as the development of equal opportunity strategies and educational programs relating to the promotion of the principle of equal pay for work of equal value.

THE 1972 EQUAL PAY DECISION

In 1972 the Australian Conciliation and Arbitration Commission extended the 1969 equal pay for equal work decision by determining that

> the concept of 'equal pay for equal work' is too narrow in today's world and we think the time has come to enlarge the concept to 'equal pay for work of equal value'. This means that award rates for all work should be considered without regard to the sex of the employee. (Equal Pay Decision Print B8506, 1972:7)

Statutory framework
Equal pay for work of equal value

AUSTRALIAN CONSTITUTION

(s 51 xxxv)
Power to enable the
conciliation and
arbitration of
industrial disputes

(s 51 xxix) External Affairs Power.
Provides power to
ratify and implement
international
conventions within
Australian domestic
law

INTERNATIONAL CONVENTIONS
UN Convention on the Elimination of
All Forms of Discrimination Against
Women (ratified 1983)
ILO Convention Equal Remuneration No 100
(ratified 1974)
ILO Convention Discrimination
(Employment and Occupation) No 111
(ratified 1973)

FEDERAL

Conciliation and Arbitration
Commission Act 1904 replaced
by Industrial Relations Act 1988

Sex Discrimination Act 1984
Human Rights and Equal
Opportunity Commission Act 1986

Affirmative Action (Equal
Employment Opportunity for
Women) Act 1986

Public Service Reform Act 1984
Merit Protection (Australian
Government Employees) Act 1984

Development of equal employment
opportunity policies and programs

STATE LEGISLATION

Industrial
NSW Industrial Arbitration Act 1940
Vic. Industrial Relation Act 1981
Qld. Industrial Conciliation &
Arbitration Act 1961
WA Industrial Relations Act 1985
SA Industrial Conciliation &
Arbitration Act 1972
Tas. Industrial Relations Act 1984

Anti-Discrimination
NSW Anti-Discrimination Act 1977
Vic. Equal Opportunity Act 1984

WA Equal Opportunity Act 1984

SA Equal Opportunity Act 1984

Other State legislation
affecting equal opportunity

Unions were to seek agreement with employers and refer to the ACAC in the event of not finding agreement. If agreement were not reached, work value inquiries were to be conducted (paragraph 4 of the 1972 Equal Pay Principle — see Appendix). The ACAC stipulated that equal pay for work of equal value be phased in in three equal instalments by June 1975.

In the rare cases where work-value inquiries were conducted, jobs were not compared for relative levels of skill, effort and responsibility. Rather, attempts were made to assess where the formerly female classifications would fit into male classifications according to similarity of work content or task. As a result, Short is able to comment, 'before 1972 male and female work was compared to see if it was exactly the same or very nearly; after 1972 work was compared to see if it was similar, looking at work content or work tasks rather than making any real attempt at valuing female work on more general criteria' (1986:325).

There appears to have been no attempt, in equal pay cases at the Commonwealth level, to compare dissimilar jobs or classifications in work-value terms (Short, 1986:325). Similarity in job *content*, not in job *value*, has been the prime concern. The dissimilar components of similar or closely related jobs were not investigated in comparative work-value terms, and neither was the possibility that similarity in work value existed in dissimilar jobs. Further, there has been no attempt to *re*assess (or assess, for that matter) the value of traditionally female work in relation to the work traditionally performed by males.

Background to the Comparable Worth Test Case, 1983–86

At the ACTU Congress in 1983 a statement was produced indicating an intention to act on the pay equity issue: 'Recognising that the value of jobs may have been set on the basis that they have historically been performed by women [the ACTU will] seek to ensure that the comparable worth of all jobs be established on a non-sexist basis' (ACTU, 1983a:4). At the same congress, the 1977 ACTU Women's Charter was amended to include the statement: 'The principle of equal pay for work of equal value should be pursued using objective criteria to ensure that predominantly or exclusively female classifications or occupations are properly valued' (ACTU, 1983b:3).

Three women's organisations — the National Council of Women of Australia, the Union of Australian Women and the Women's Electoral Lobby (WEL) — intervened in the 1983 *National Wage Case* and submitted that the implementation of the 1972 ruling had not been accompanied by proper work-value exercises. WEL asked that a reintroduced central wage-fixing system make provision for a new evaluation of this work (WEL, 1983). The Full Bench rejected the submission on the grounds that

> We consider that such large work value inquiries would clearly provide an opportunity for the development of additional tiers of wage increases which would be inconsistent with the centralised system which we propose for the next two years and would also be inappropriate in the current state of unemployment especially among women. Moreover, many of the problems which the WEL has raised are a matter for management, unions and governments rather than for award provision. (National Wage Decision Print F2900, 1983:29)

In September 1984 the ACTU adopted an Action Program for Women Workers, based on the policy developments of the previous year, and in it set out strategies for the next two years to improve the position of females in the labour market. The strategies included the intention to pursue a comparable worth claim before the ACAC. It was intended to examine the feasibility of applying the comparable worth principle by first testing it with an occupation such as nursing and, if necessary, seeking changes in the wage-fixing principles (ACTU, 1984:9).

Comparable worth was defined in the following way:

> an employee's earnings should be based on [the] knowledge, skill, effort, responsibility and so on his/her work requires relative to other work, regardless of whether the work is undertaken by males or females.
> Comparable worth or pay equity has not been fully applied in Australia which may mean there is still sex bias in the earnings of some traditionally female occupations, resulting in those tradition-ally female occupations being under-valued. (ACTU, 1985:26)

In 1985 the ACTU lodged a test case on the issue of 'equal pay for work of equal value' which it equated with 'comparable worth'. The award being dealt with was the Private Hospitals' and Doctors' Nurses (ACT) Award, 1972. The ACTU sought a reaffirmation of the 1972 Equal Pay decision and a ruling that it was still available to be implemented. On establishing the ACAC's view through an in-principle determination, the ACTU was then planning to introduce the concept into a review of the wage-fixing principles, due later in the year.

The ACTU proposed to compare the knowledge, skill, effort, responsibility and working conditions experienced by nurses with the work requirements and conditions of the male-dominated occupations of ambulance officers, firemen, aircraft ground engineers, and metal trades fitters. It proposed an 'objective' points-score assessment of the comparative value of the work done in the different occupations as a means of determining the appropriate wage increases for nurses (DEIR, 1985:10).

The ACAC's ruling of 18 February 1986, however, was not sympathetic to the concept of comparable worth. Indeed, it criticised the concept as being 'quite contrary to what the Full Bench of the Commission envisaged in the 1972 Equal Pay Principle':

> The Principle requires equal pay for work of equal value to be implemented by work value enquiries carried out in the normal manner in which such enquires are conducted in our wage fixing environment. This is clear from the methods of comparison laid down in paragraph 5 of the Principle. In addition subparagraph (c) of paragraph 5 specifically rejects the assessment of the work on the basis of its value to the employer ... (Arb. Comm. Print G2250, 1986:6)

The ACAC also said that the comparable worth approach would 'strike at the heart of long accepted methods of wage fixation in this country and would be particularly destructive of the present Wage Fixing principles'. One of the reasons for this assertion is made clear in another statement of the ACAC, where the concept of comparable worth is understood as having a general application, rather than as a principle to be used to redress women's lower rates of pay. The latter is the situation in Canada, for example (see Cadieux, 1984). In Ontario, a province which has introduced pay equity legislation covering the private sector, the Pay Equity Commissioner said: 'The goal of pay equity is clear—equitable pay for workers doing jobs traditionally performed by women' (Podrebarac, 1987:1).

But the Full Bench of the ACAC stated:

> At its widest, comparable worth is capable of being applied to any classification regarded as having been improperly valued, without limitation on the kind of classification to which it is applied, with no requirement that the work performed is related or similar. It is capable of being applied to work which is essentially or usually performed by females. (Arb. Comm. Print G2250, 1986:6)

This apparent contradiction in attitude on the part of the ACAC—extending the meaning of equal pay in 1972 on the one hand and on the other warning of the industrial upheaval that might result from its application—achieves an uneasy resolution in the ACAC's decision that the implementation of the 1972 decision is subject to the constraints of the Anomalies provision of the wage-fixing principles.

Paragraph (a)(i) of provision 6, Anomalies and Inequities as set out in the National Wage Case of 1983, stated:

> In the resolution of anomalies, the overriding concept is that the Commission must be satisfied that any claim under this Principle will not be a vehicle for general improvements in pay and con-

ditions and that the circumstances warranting the improvement are of a special and isolated nature. (National Wage Decision Print F2900, 1983:51)

Just as importantly, perhaps, the ACAC ruled that the 1972 decision is still available to be implemented, but implied that this was the case only for awards where it has not yet been implemented (Arb. Comm. Print G2250, 1986:7). It may be that what the ACAC meant here is 'not yet adequately, properly implemented'. In an equal pay case brought for arbitration by the Municipal Officers' Association in Tasmania, Deputy President Isaac said:

the equal pay concept underlying the 1972 principles was a landmark in the history of arbitration in Australia and its proper application should be supported by the Commission. The implementation of equal pay by consent and in good faith is not immutable, even after a substantial time lapse, if it can be shown that the implementation was not in accordance with the principles. (Arb. Comm. Print E 7900, 1981:19)

The Council of Action for Equal Pay went further in its submission to the comparable worth hearing, arguing that the rates of pay for all women in predominantly female occupations, including those which had already had the 1972 Principle applied to their rates of pay, should be reassessed case by case (Arb. Comm. Print G2250, 1986:6).

In March 1987 the ACAC handed down the *National Wage Case Decision* (Print G6800) implementing a new two-tier system to be reviewed again in 1988. The Anomalies and Inequities provision was retained (as it had been in the *National Wage Case* of 1986, Print G3600, 1986:77) and was the provision under which equal pay claims could still be made.

Pay cases relating to female-dominated occupational groups brought before the ACAC, 1985−88

1 *The Nurses' Case* The ACAC determined, in its decision of 18 February 1986 on the nurses' claim for salary increases, that:

From the material that was put to us it appears that all parties acknowledge that a number of special factors may be relevant to a review of nurses' salaries. It is our view that the pursuit of this claim through the Anomalies Conference should involve the raising of all those issues ... (Arb. Comm. Print G2250, 1986:7−8)

The Anomalies Conference dealing with the nurses' case was held in March 1986 and the ACTU presented a detailed argument on a number of special factors relevant to the nurses' situation and wages. It was not just an equal pay case. The case was brought during a time of nurse shortage, the training of nurses was moving from hospitals to colleges of advanced education, there was a concern to establish a proper career structure, and there were claims for significant changes in work value.

But in relation to the application of the 1972 Equal Pay decision, the ACTU

> tabled an exhaustive history of the ACT Public Sector nurses' wage movements, and a comparison of the separate and cumulative percentage wage movements of nurses and a traditionally male occupation, metal tradesmen, in the ACT public sector over the period 1/1/71 to 15/5/75 to demonstrate that nurses had not received an equal pay for work of equal value wage adjustment. (ACTU, 1987:11)

On 2 April 1986 the decision of the Anomalies Conference was announced, stating that an arguable case exists and referring the claims to the Full Bench (cited in Arb. Comm. Print G7200, 1987:2).

The decision of the Full Bench was handed down on 7 May 1987 and dealt, among other things, with the claim that the 1972 Equal Pay Principle had not been applied in the awards being considered. The decision stated that:

> All of the indications ... point to a situation of no positive application of the 1972 decision in any of the consent settlements in the Commonwealth area. An examination of wage rates in the ACT, for example, indicates no advance since 1972 by nurses as compared with male tradesmen. In our opinion all that has happened is that differences between male and female rates within nurse awards have been eliminated, but the original sex bias caused by assessment on the basis of a predominantly female rate remains. As the wage history of all Commonwealth nurses reveals a link with the fixation for ACT nurses in 1970 the non-application of the 1972 Equal Pay decision applies in respect of all awards and determinations before us.
>
> This situation, as it applies to nurses, in our view is a special and isolated factor and we think it unlikely that there are many occupations in which, in 1987, wages are still depressed because of the non-application of the 1972 decision. (Arb. Comm. Print G7200, 1987:12)

2   *The Therapists' Case*   At the same time that the ACTU was preparing its Comparable Worth Test Case, another case was being prepared by the Professional Officers' Association (POA), Australian Public Service, on behalf of physiotherapists, occupational therapists and speech pathologists in the APS. The case for equal pay with other similarly qualified science professionals was argued under the Anomalies provision of the prevailing (1983) Wage Fixing Principles. It did not receive the same attention as the nurses' case, not being set up to test the comparable worth principle.

The non-application of the 1969 and 1972 Equal Pay decisions was acknowledged by agreement between the parties in document-ation submitted to the Anomalies Full Bench (Felicity Rafferty, pers. comm.).

It was claimed by the POA in Submissions that the three occupa-tions should be paid the same rates of pay as those applying to the science group, which is a broad category encompassing all occupa-tions requiring a minimum qualification of a three-year degree in science. It was submitted that the therapist occupations met the criteria for inclusion in the science group in relation to the nature of work performed and qualification requirements, but that the National Wage Principles precluded the employer from incorporating the therapist occupations into the group. The Public Service Board sub-mitted that the alignment sought by the POA had been actively considered in the early 1980s, but that the Board had not been satisfied in the circumstances existing at the time that including them in the science category was justified. The POA submitted that it was anomalous that the therapists had been refused entry to the science group in the past because they were unable to meet the criteria, yet when the criteria were able to be met the employer was unable to act because of constraints imposed by the National Wage Principles (Felicity Rafferty, pers. comm.).

The Full Bench decision on the matter indicated that it was satisfied that the position of therapists was anomalous and that 'there is no longer any justification for excluding them from the Science group of employees in the Australian Public Service' (Arb. Comm. Print G1499, 1985:2).

3 The Social Workers' Case A third case involves social workers employed by the APS, the resolution of which was announced on 14 April 1988. The case, taken to the ACAC by the POA once more, was dealt with before the Anomalies Conference under the Inequities provision of the 1987 Wage Fixing Principles. This provision states, among other things, that the only claims that can be made under it are claims relating to classes of work that 'are truly like with like as to all relevant matters and there is no good reason for dissimilar rates of pay' (National Wage Decision, Print G6800, 1987:40).

The case involved a claim that there was an inequity in the salary rates applying to social workers on the one hand and counsellors on the other, on the basis of 'objective classification criteria which have regard to the nature of the work, skill and responsibility required and the conditions under which the work is performed'. The counsellor classification was introduced into the APS in 1977 and its rates were determined by the Public Service Board to equate with the rates for psychologists at Classes 1–3. The case is complex, and not all the arguments raised in relation to the Wage Fixing Principles are dealt with here. Suffice it to say that the female-dominated classification of social worker was indirectly compared with the male-dominated classification of psychologist through the claim of like work with the female-dominated and, numerically speaking, relatively small classification of counsellor.

As far as the POA is concerned, the case was a victory on pay equity grounds for a female-dominated occupational group. The claim was initiated under the Anomalies provision, and the POA sought application of the 1972 Equal Pay Principle for this predominantly female profession. It used as part of its evidence of non-application the fact that the social workers' five-class professional structure was the lowest paid in Commonwealth employment, and it furnished evidence of the identical nature of the skills, knowledge and work of social workers employed under two different awards (covering social workers on the one hand and counsellors on the other, the category of counsellor covering both psychologists and social workers performing identical work) where different rates of pay applied.

The claim was resolved by agreement under the Inequities and not the Anomalies provision, and the Anomalies Conference confirmed that the functions and duties performed by social workers 'are truly like with like in all relevant respects to those performed by counsellors' (National Wage Case Conference of Anomalies, Transcript of Proceedings, 14 April 1988:2).

Comment on the cases

In the nurses' case the decision to award pay increases was related to so many factors that it is impossible to determine the proportion which might be attributed to an adjustment on the grounds of non-application of the 1972 Equal Pay Principle. And it is clear, in the decision, that the amount of pay increase was very much a matter of matching what had already been determined by State tribunals: 'we have been given [no] information or material which would justify a fixation of rates beyond the levels of the rates for nurses which have been assessed by recent decisions of State tribunals' (Arb. Comm. Print G7200, 1987:25).

'Equal pay for work of equal value' can mean many things, depending on the criteria of value chosen. The statement of the Full Bench in the therapists' case placed heavy emphasis on educational qualifications rather than on work-level descriptions as expressions of job demands. It drew attention, at some length, to entrance requirements, course duration and curriculum content (Arb. Comm. Print G1499, 1985:2) despite the fact that the criteria set up to determine what constitutes scientific work include questions of job demands. And the statement of the Full Bench makes no reference to the non-application of the 1972 Equal Pay Principle, so that the case became, in effect, a consideration of the implications of the apparent changes in the nature of the educational qualifications gained by therapists since about 1973. It was on these grounds that an Anomaly was found, rather than on the grounds of the non-application of the 1972 Equal Pay Principle.

In the social workers' case the emphasis was the other way around. Because it was resolved under the Inequities provision, the issue was whether the work of the social workers was the same as the work of the counsellors, and a great deal of attention was given to the actual work performed. The non-application of the 1972 Equal Pay Principle, an important part of the initial claim put by the POA, was not a matter for determination. The agreement that was reached is correctly cited as 'another landmark in the implementation of equal pay' and an advance 'against sexual discrimination in professional pay rates' (Grey, 1988:1), but is nevertheless not one which applies the 1972 equal pay for work of equal value ruling.

The POA has identified the occupations of librarians, audiologists and dental therapists as other predominantly female professions requiring pay equity action. Under the existing restraints placed on what is determined to be an Anomaly, and the restrictions placed on cases brought under the Inequities provision, we will no doubt find the POA launching cases as carefully as they did the previous two. But there is no immediate or obvious answer to the question of what argument might successfully be put for shop assistants, secretaries, female process production workers, childcare workers, clerical workers and other predominantly female occupational groups which cannot rely on demonstrations of 'like' work or on comparable educational qualifications.

There are numerous criteria used for comparative purposes in the ACAC decisions which reflect ideas about the value, and thus the relative value, of different kinds of work. Presumably the criteria used in work-value cases in the past could be drawn on to determine 'equal value'. But it would appear that the selection from the wide range of criteria has a lot to do with the ACAC's assessment of the likely future impact of such selections, particularly flow-on effects.

For example, as part of the case made for the previous non-application of the 1972 Equal Pay Principle, the ACTU and the Royal Australian Nursing Federation (RANF) claimed 'that nurses should now be accorded the professional status which hitherto had been denied them' (Arb. Comm. Print G7200, 1987:25), but the ACAC regarded this as going 'well beyond the application of the 1972 decision', both because they were not convinced by the ACTU or the

RANF of the need to move to professional rates, 'whatever that term may mean', and because it questioned whether such a move could be justified during the transitional period of the change to full-time CAE nurse education, and particularly 'while we have no means of comparing the worth of the diploma with the qualifications obtained by other professional employees operating within the health care industry' (Arb. Comm. Print G7200, 1987:25). Yet in the Professional Engineers' Case, when referring to the fixing of salary rates for a Grade 1 engineer, the ACAC said:

> We think that the work is truly professional, that whether the profession is entered by way of a degree course or diploma course intensive study is required, that this study must be such as will enable an employee to acquire the knowledge of higher mathematics necessary for dealing with complex engineering problems; that notwithstanding the existence of supervision, a Grade 1 engineer carries the responsibilities of professional duties and that in practice he [sic] performs useful and essential work as a member of a team. (Comm. Arb. Reports 1961, vol. 97:325)

The problem referred to in the Nurses' Case is in fact not an unfamiliar one to the ACAC, and one to which it has applied solutions in the past. Indeed, Deputy President Isaac, in a ruling on pay rates for bank officers, indicated that assessing relative educational qualifications and training requirements is a normal practice:

> The determination of relative work requirements is necessarily a matter of judgment. There are cases where no comparable job exists and resort must be had to comparing formal qualifications and training requirements, at least as an important element in determining the value of work. (Arb. Comm. Print C4578, 1975:2)

Can pay equity be reached?

'Pay equity' is a term generally regarded as having broader application than 'comparable worth' because of the number of strategies that might be implemented that contribute towards it. As the ACAC has observed, some of these are matters for management, unions and government.

But the issue which remains central to comparable worth strategies and pay equity advocates is the evidence that traditional female classifications are paid less because work that women do is regarded as less valuable than work that men do; that criteria of value, however formalised, contain a degree of 'masculine bias' which needs to be eliminated if the value of women's work is to be adequately assessed and remunerated. This is why the cases dealt with above, as important as they are as pay equity strategies, are of limited usefulness for the overall situation of women in predominantly female classifications. Women workers need to have the specific qualities and skills demanded by the jobs they perform first acknowledged as elements to be considered in work-value assessments, and then, of course, remunerated equitably.

The ACAC stated, in its decision of 18 February 1986, that in the submission before it, 'there was no analysis of this Commission's decisions or the methods by which rates are fixed in its awards or determinations to indicate that these inequalities were reflected in award rates of pay' (Arb. Comm. Print G2250:6). As the ACAC has stated many times, the determination of work value involves the exercise of judgment; there is no 'objective' way of determining it. The ACAC is right: research evidence is of subjectivity and systematic gender bias in all conventional job classification and evaluation systems (for a review of this literature and its findings, see Burton et al., 1987).

For example, it has already been pointed out that formal qualifications and training requirements are frequently used as important elements in determining the value of work, in cases where there are no comparable jobs for determining relative work requirements. Yet many of the skills and qualities women bring to their jobs have developed outside formal training and educational courses and institutions (for example, machine-sewing, cooking, childcare, personal service work, manual dexterity).

In line with the ACAC's statement on the determination of work value, that 'different criteria will continue to apply from case to case and may vary from one class of work to another' (*Equal Pay Decision*, Print B8506, 1972:8), it would appear that, in some cases of women's work, emphasis needs to be placed on job demands and on-the-job training rather than on formal educational qualifications so that the qualities and skills women bring to jobs and accumulate there have attention drawn to them.

The implications of such an approach were drawn out in the decisions in the *Metal Trades Award Work Value Inquiry* (Arb. Comm. Print B2916, 1967), where it was stated, in relation to female process workers:

> They have no trade qualifications and in general they handle machines the operation of which calls for manual dexterity rather than technical skill. Let it not be thought, however, that their value as employees is to be deprecated. They keep up with fast producing machines, their work requires close concentration, they are production minded, their productivity is high.
> ... as a generalisation it may be said that a period of two months elapses before full efficiency is attained ... an indication of manual dexterity may be sought before an employee is engaged (Justice Gallagher, p. 743).

> ... process workers ... work constantly, often at a pace set for them and are required to complete complex and pernickety jobs which require some degree of attention. The work done by some is on components so small that a microscope has to be used ... The process worker must be manually dextrous and in many cases must be able to perform more than one function. They must accept some responsibility for their work and in some instances make the final check of a product (Justice Moore, p. 754).
>
> ... there was some ground for considering ... that with regard to the process workers working in the domain of the miniature in electronic and electrical component processing, the female was more valuable than the male in certain classifications (Commissioner Winter, p. 796).
>
> In this domain it is not too much to say that the reality is that the female process worker usually warrants a higher wage than her male counterpart (Commissioner Winter, p. 888).

Our knowledge of job demands on workers is developing in ways that bring greater recognition to those experienced by women. For example, knowledge has accumulated of the physical stress and fatigue involved in many women's jobs. A hand-and-eye coordination job often requires more energy, more effort, more concentration, and is more taxing than work of men lifting something that weighs 35lbs every ten minutes (Rubenstein, 1984:98). Similarly,

> Men's jobs frequently receive extra points for the strength required in occasionally lifting heavy weights in comparison with women who may repeatedly lift light weights. Different results might follow if this factor was measured by total weight lifted per work day or according to total caloric output expended. (Rubenstein, 1984:98)

Qualities and skills demanded of predominantly female positions have been detailed extensively in the literature (see Burton et al., 1987). But clear illustrations can be readily presented of qualities and skills which are frequently overlooked in the assessment of women's work. The pamphlet *Questions and Answers: pay equity in the workplace*, published to prepare employers and unions for the impact of the pay equity legislation in Ontario, Canada, points to some of these (See chapter 8).

But to what classification or occupation are women's positions to be compared? Other female classifications are likely to have job demands that have gone unacknowledged as well. To compare them with similar or dissimilar male classifications will do nothing to remedy the situation unless particular attention is drawn to the previously unacknowledged job demands or the fact of their under-valuation. Then they are able to be recognised as additional to, or different from but of some relative value to, the job demands within the male classifications used for comparative purposes.

This is a familiar problem to the ACAC. Deputy President Isaac, in a decision on the pay of bank officers, said:

> as I understand it, the work value principle requires that, other things being equal, persons doing the same work should be paid the same wage; those doing similar work should be remunerated similarly; and those doing different jobs should have their pay proportioned, as far as this is possible, to the volume and standard of job requirements. Thus comparative wage justice underlies the determination of work value. (Arb. Comm. Print C4578, 1975:2)

And, we hope, would determine the monetary value to be placed on the outcome of work-value reassessments.

The phrasing of paragraph 5(b) of the 1972 Equal Pay decision (see Appendix) is designed, as far as possible, to restrict the range of jobs which can be drawn on for comparative purposes to those which are closely related or similar (the definition of 'similar' work is not clear in several ACAC rulings; the preference in this paragraph for female rather than male classifications in other awards privileges a certain form of 'similarity'). This is a restriction which goes beyond the actual practice of the ACAC, since, in some cases before it, comparisons were made of predominantly male classifications with predominantly male classifications in other awards in other industries (perhaps because they appear similar on the grounds that men perform in the positions).

The exercise of broad judgment and the choice of comparable jobs for the determination of relative work-value requirements appears to have been more flexible in some decisions not involving equal pay claims than paragraph 5(b) of the 1972 Equal Pay Principle would allow. It would appear that there have been different applications of the 'equal pay for work of equal value' principle and that the application of it has been to the advantage of predominantly male classifications. It has been applied more narrowly and less flexibly with respect to predominantly female classifications.

According to Short (1986:323), the journalists' case 'is the only case before 1972 where comparison of dissimilar work was openly acknowledged in setting pay levels'. The ACAC, in this case, compared journalists with public servants and teachers, finding the former suitable for comparative purposes:

> It cannot be disputed that journalism differs from other professions or avocations. Nevertheless we do not think we should attempt to consider salaries for journalists in an industrial or social vacuum. We think it proper in this professional area to look both at present salaries and past movements in salaries of employees with comparable educational qualifications who are called upon to display similar qualities in their work even though the work itself is dissimilar. (Arb. Comm. Print B3900, 1967:4)

In an ACAC hearing on pay for bank officers (Arb. Comm. Print C4578, 1975), which was heard after the 1972 Equal Pay decision, the submission of the Australian Bank Officials' Association drew comparisons between the 21-year-old bank officer and the base-grade clerk in the APS. It also compared officers at higher levels with Class 8 administrative/clerical officers in the APS, while acknowledging the difficulties in comparison given the special nature of banking work. In his decision, Isaac accepted the validity of such comparison; he was

> satisfied that on the job descriptions, initial qualifications and on-the-job training requirements put to me ... the pay increases would not over-value the work of bank officers, certainly at the lower levels of the work hierarchy, At the higher levels, *from my knowledge of work performed in the Australian Public Service*, I would not regard the ... proposed pay of the top level manager as excessive. (Arb. Comm. Print C4578, 1985:2, italics added)

Paragraph 5(b) of the 1972 Equal Pay Principle needs to be interpreted to become more in line with the commitment of the ACAC to the 'broad judgment which has characterised work value enquiries'. It needs to be brought into line the ACAC's practice, as illustrated in the cases above. If the 1972 Principle is to achieve what it intended to achieve pay equity for women worker then such practice needs to be regarded as reasonable in the choice of comparative jobs for the determination of relative work value of women's jobs.

Pay equity for women workers, a concept with a wider meaning than that given to 'comparable worth', requires an application of the 'equal pay for work of equal value' principle which would allow for a comparison of the work value of jobs performed within predominantly female occupations and classifications with that of jobs performed within predominantly male occupations and classifications. The focus of any system or strategy that is devised needs to be on such comparison within awards, across awards within the same enterprise, across awards within the same industry, and across industries for similar kinds of work (as in the two cases cited above).

Whatever other considerations then come to be applied, that male-female comparative focus would remain the basis for the application of the 1972 Equal Pay Principle, since it is what pay equity strategies for women imply, based as they are on the evidence of the lower relative value placed on work that is performed predominantly by women.

None of the wage-fixing principles devised over the last fifteen or so years has facilitated the implementation of the 1972 Principle. For it to contribute to pay equity for women, its application to date would need to be reviewed. Paragraph 5(a) has not, on the whole, been applied. In those cases where 'consideration of the work performed' has not occurred, and in those cases where it has, but improperly, a further inquiry into work value should be conducted. It would be appropriate that, in such inquiries, the accumulated knowledge of how sex bias might intrude in the analysis, description and evaluation of predominantly women's jobs should be taken into account.

It would also seem that any new initiative relating to sex bias in wage-setting procedures would need to incorporate the requirement that job evaluation systems (given their widespread use within enterprises) be examined for such bias. Employers and the consultants in the various firms delivering schemes to client enterprises would then be under an obligation to ensure that all steps had been taken to eliminate sex bias from the design and implementation of a scheme.

With such an initiative, whether it be legislative or through the industrial relations machinery, wage-fixing bodies would have an obligation, in the first place, to assess any proposed job evaluation system agreed to in a restructured award to be certain that it does not have sex bias built into its design, and that appropriate procedures are agreed upon as far as bias-free implementation processes are concerned. Indeed, given the impact of apparently 'neutral' organisational processes on those with a relative lack of power to influence them, the central body would no doubt be seeking ways of ensuring that the process is one which actively seeks to ensure that women's skills and qualities are acknowledged and equitably remunerated.

In the second place, a wage-fixing body, in line with the recommendation contained in the WEL submission to the 1983 *National Wage Case* (WEL, 1983:59), would have an obligation to set up appropriate machinery, such as through the appointment of a panel of commissioners to deal with work-value inquiries for women workers (or through setting up a pay equity unit with the ACAC to be used as a resource by the commissioners). Such a move would aim to ensure that, in any work-value inquiry, the range of skills and qualities women bring to their work, and the range of job demands to which they respond in their job performance, would, again, be acknowledged and equitably remunerated.

In these circumstances, it would be left to the commissioners to decide whether it would be useful, in a particular work-value inquiry, to apply a formal job evaluation method to help determine whether dissimilar work is similar in work-value terms. The commissioners would obviously be concerned that any method used was demonstrated to be free of sex bias. In this way, job evaluation methods might not only prove useful from time to time, but the firms offering their job evaluation services would have an interest in ensuring that they have eliminated any possible sex bias from their schemes. Such a situation might also promote the development of new job evaluation methods and schemes, designed specifically to ensure that job factors and their weightings reflect more adequately than is the case in schemes currently in use women's typical job demands and the qualities and skills women use in response to them.

THE CONSEQUENCES OF THE INTRODUCTION OF EQUAL PAY

The wage gap

Statistical data on the male—female wage ratio for 1969—75 is used below to demonstrate the effects of the implementation of the 1969 and 1972 equal pay decisions as well as the effect of the 1974 decision to extend the male adult minimum wage to adult women. Commentators use the range of average hourly and weekly earnings for ordinary and total time, for full-time and for all employees.

Whatever data is used, and whatever the reasons for using different sets of data (some of which are discussed below), the overall pattern of relative wage rates is clear. The 1969 ruling benefited about 18 per cent of the female workforce, that being the proportion outside female-dominated classifications which could take advantage of the 'equal pay for equal work' ruling. Many more women benefited from the combined effects of the 1972 and 1974 decisions, the latter, obviously, being particularly significant for low-income-earning women (see Ryan and Conlon, 1975; WEL, 1983; O'Donnell and Hall, 1988).

Table 1 below shows the female-to-male ratio of hourly earnings and ordinary-time earnings, 1972—84. Table 2 shows the female-to-male ratio of earnings for full-time workers, 1972—87.

When part-time workers are included, women earned 60 cents for every dollar which males earned in 1972; in 1981 that figures was 67 cents (WEL, 1983:7). For the August quarter 1987 this figure was 66 cents (ABS Average Weekly Earnings, States and Australia, August 1987, Cat. No. 6302.0). By 1976, the increase in the female—male ratio appeared to level out. The slight movements since then, up and down, can be related to events within the industrial relations arena (See O'Donnell and Hall; 1988:60; Ryan, 1988:13).

It appears that under the two-tier wage-fixing system which arose from the March 1987 National Wage Case Decision (Arb. Comm. Print Q6800, 1987) women did not increase their wage rates as much as their male counterparts, even though the system was supposed to benefit low-paid women in particular.

At the beginning of 1987, women's wages rose at a greater rate than men's as a result of the $10 flat-rate increase awarded to all workers. But, according to ABS figures, between May and August,

Table 1 Female-to-male ratio of hourly earnings and ordinary-time earnings, 1972–84 (October–November): full-time adult non-managerial employees

	Average hourly earnings	Average hourly ordinary-time earnings
1972	74.2	76.0
1973	76.1	78.5
1974	79.9	82.3
1975	83.7	85.8
1976	85.7	87.5
1977	86.5	88.2
1978	86.8	88.2
1979	85.5	87.6
1980	86.0	88.3
1981	N/A	84.3
1982	82.9	84.5
1983	85.0	83.5
1984	85.6	87.5

Source: Table 3.1 in O'Donnell and Hall, 1988:50

Table 2 Full-time workers: ratio of female to male earnings

Year	Earnings Males $	Females $	Ratio
1972	106.0	69.0	.65
1973	115.0	81.0	.70
1974	157.0	112.0	.71
1975	159.0	121.0	.76
1976	182.0	141.0	.78
1977	200.0	157.0	.79
1978	220.0	174.0	.79
1979	235.0	185.0	.79
1980	261.0	208.0	.80
1981	289.0	232.0	.80
1982	335.0	261.0	.78
1983	370.0	286.0	.77
1984	401.0	311.0	.77
1985	429.0	336.0	.78
1986	460.0	360.0	.78
1987	489.0	384.2	.79

Source: ABS Average Weekly Earnings (February series) Cat. No.6302.0

full-time adult male average weekly ordinary-time earnings rose by 2.3 per cent, while the women's average increased by 1.7 per cent. Between August and November 1987, the equivalent male figure was 1.6 per cent and the female figure 0.8 per cent (ABS, *Average Weekly Earnings, States and Australia*, August and November 1987, Cat. No. 6302.0). For the year February 1987 to February 1988, full-time adult male average weekly ordinary-time earnings increased by 6.9 per cent, and for the equivalent females, by 6.7 per cent (ABS, *Average Weekly Earnings, Australia*, February 1988, Preliminary, Cat. No 6301.0).

The concern of pay equity advocates is that different wage-fixing principles, and the development of different criteria by which wage increases can be claimed, have different effects on the wages of men and women, For example, Jennie George argues that the 1987 Restructuring and Efficiency provision 'was being increasingly interpreted as straight productivity bargaining. This left women at a disadvantage in second tier bargaining, because they were not clustered in areas of market based productivity' (cited in Women's Bureau, 1988b:3). And Meredith Burgmann argues:

> Women are being penalised because they lack ... organisation and inbuilt work practices to bargain with. Large numbers of them are in the service areas, which are difficult to quantify, and in retailing, where there's no fat to trim off. As a result they'll miss out on the 4 per cent rise, or get it late. (cited in Powell, 1988:11)

An overall assessment of this situation is yet to be carried out.

Employment opportunities

We need to consider, too, whether there is a discernible effect of the equal pay decisions on employment opportunities for women. Gregory and Ho (1985; see also Gregory and Duncan, 1981) argue that there has not been an effect on the 'relative rate of growth of female to male hours supplied to the economy' (1985:29) and they point out that 'the unemployment of women in Australia has continued to fall relative to that of men and also appears not to have been affected to a great degree (1985:31). They do, however, suggest that the larger increase in part-time jobs in Australia than in the United States might be attributable to the history of relative pay changes. These authors argue that the sex segregation of the workforce reduced the possibility that the equal pay decisions would have a negative effect on the share of jobs offered to women in the labour market.

These last two points particularly concern McGavin (1983). He claims that the equal pay decision had the effects one would expect, at least from a 'neo-classical theoretical perspective': 'changes in relative factor prices will generate changes in relative factor combinations' (McGavin, 1983:48). He believes that Gregory and associates have over-estimated the role of the sex-segregated nature of the labour market in acting as a barrier to substitution responses to relative wage changes.

McGavin supplies an interpretation of the impact of the equal pay decisions using hours of employment data and a comparison between data from government and market sectors of the economy. The results of his analysis, McGavin claims, 'document the significant role of increased part-time employment for the changes in women's employment' and suggests that 'this variation in the pattern of employment has a timing suggestive of an equal pay influence' (1983:58). He believes these results also make clearer the importance of the growth of non-market sector employment for the change in female employment in Australia.

A realistic assessment of cause-effect sequences is difficult. We need to consider a range of factors when we look at employment patterns for men and women. Industry restructuring from around 1974 in response to economic recession is one. Job losses were occurring in manufacturing while jobs, both full-and part-time, were being created in service industries. Another consideration is the impact of the policies of the Labor Government in the period 1972–75, when funding to health, education and welfare, areas of women's employment, was increased.

In August 1987 39 per cent of women worked part-time compared with 7.4 per cent of men, and 78 per cent of part-time workers were women. Moreover,

> part-time employment is increasing faster than full-time, and the increase in part-time work for women was the most important contribution to total net employment growth in the period 1973–83. Over half the new jobs created since 1973 have been part-time, and women have gained 60 per cent of the new jobs. (O'Donnell and Hall, 1988:31)

The proportion of the increase in part-time work which can be attributable to the effects of the equal pay decisions is not at all clear. McGavin (1983) attempts such an estimate. But as Gregory and Ho point out, 'the economic literature may not have paid sufficient attention to the effects of non-economic factors upon [employment patterns] and relative wages of men and women' (1985:34).

Appendix: The 1972 Equal Pay Principle

1 The principle of 'equal pay for work of equal value' will be applied to all awards of the Commission. By 'equal pay for work of equal value' we mean the fixation of award rates by a consideration of the work performed irrespective of the sex of the worker. The principle will apply to both adults and juniors. Because the male minimum wage takes account of family considerations it will not apply to females.

2 Adoption of the new principle requires that female rates be determined by work value comparisons without regard to the sex of the employees concerned. Differentiations between male rates in awards of the Commission have traditionally been founded on work value investigations of various occupational groups or classifications. The gap between the level of male and female rates in awards generally is greater than the gap, if any, in the comparative value of work performed by the two sexes because rates for female classifications in the same award have generally been fixed without a comparative evaluation of the work performed by males and females.

3 The new principle may be applied by agreement or arbitration. The eventual outcome should be a single rate for an occupational group or classification which rate is payable to the employee performing the work whether the employee be male or female. Existing geographical differences between rates will not be affected by this decision.

4 Implementation of the new principle by arbitration will call for the exercise of the broad judgment which has characterised work value inquiries. Different criteria will continue to apply from case to case and may vary from one class of work to another. However, work value inquiries which are concerned with comparisons of work and fixation of award rates irrespective of the sex of employees may encounter unfamiliar issues. In so far as those issues have been raised

we will comment on them. Other issues which may arise will be resolved in the context of the particular work value inquiry with which the arbitration is concerned.

5 We now deal with issues which have arisen from the material and argument placed before us and which call for comment or decision.

(a) The automatic application of any formula which seeks to by-pass a consideration of the work performed is, in our view, inappropriate to the implementation of the principles we have adopted. However, pre-existing award relativities may be a relevant factor in appropriate cases.

(b) Work value comparisons should, where possible, be made between female and male classifications within the award under consideration. But where such comparisons are unavailable or inconclusive, as may be the case where the work is performed exclusively by females, it may be necessary to take into account comparisons of work value between female classifications within the award and/or comparisons of work value between female classifications in different awards. In some cases comparisons with male classifications in other awards may be necessary.

(c) The value of the work refers to worth in terms of award wage or salary fixation, not worth to the employer.

(d) Although a similarity in name may indicate a similarity of work, it may be found on closer examination that the same name has been given to different work. In particular, this situation may arise with generic classifications. A similar situation may arise with respect to junior employees. Whether in such circumstances it is appropriate to establish new classifications or categories will be a matter for the arbitrator.

(e) In consonance with normal work value practice it will be for the arbitrator to determine whether differences in the work performed are sufficiently significant to warrant a differentiation in rate and if so what differentiation is appropriate. It will also be for the arbitrator to determine whether restrictions on the performance of work by females under a particular award warrant any differentiation in rate based on the relative value of the work. We should however indicate that claims for differentiation based on labour turnover or absenteeism should be rejected.

(f) The new principle will have no application to the minimum wage for adult males which is determined on factors unrelated to the nature of the work performed.

6 Both the social and economic consequences of our decision will be considerable and implementation will take some time. It is our intention that rates in all awards of this Commission and all determinations under the *Public Service Arbitration Act* should have been

fixed in accordance with this decision by 30 June 1975. Under normal circumstances, implementation should take place by three equal instalments so that one-third of any increase is payable no later than 31 December 1973, half of the remainder by 30 September 1974 and the balance by 30 June 1975. This programme is intended as a norm and we recognise that special circumstances may exist which require special treatment.

7 Nothing we have said is intended to rescind the 1969 principles applicable to equal pay for equal work which will continue to apply in appropriate cases. We have taken this step because an injustice might be created in cases based on equal pay for equal work where females could become entitled immediately to male rates under those principles.

(Equal Pay Decision Print B8506, 1972)

Endnotes

Introduction

1 The *Public Service Reform Act* and the State Acts referred to above also provide for the promotion of equal employment opportunities for people with disabilities, people of Aboriginal and Torres Strait Island descent and people of non-English-speaking background.

Gender bias in job evaluation

1 For a detailed examination of the different types of job evaluation methods, see chapters 4 and 5 in Elizur (1987) and Livy (1988b).

2 Section 11 of the Canadian *Human Rights Commission Act* 1977; the United Kingdom *Equal Pay (Amendment) Regulations* 1983.

3 A sample of positions representative of those found within the organisation is chosen as a 'benchmark' sample. As far as possible, positions are chosen which are well understood and which exist in similar organisations, so that the points scores awarded to them can be used as the basis for a salary policy that is realistic in relation to market rates.

4 For more detailed discussion of the ways in which gender bias enters the position description writing and the evaluation processes, see Burton et al., 1987.

5 In this section the work of McArthur (1985) is drawn on in the identification of types of bias.

6 These quotations are taken from comments made in two Australian organisations by members of evaluation committees to which the author had access.

7 The expectation of change is higher, of course, in the situation where job evaluation systems are brought in to deal with a claim of unequal pay for work of equal value.

8 For example, if responsibilities relating to financial management give some jobs a higher score for accountability, but traditionally the jobs involved have been classified at the same level as other clerical positions without such responsibilities, there may be pressure felt within the evaluation committee to lower the score on another factor (see Burton et al., 1987:53).

9 Equal treatment, including access to benefits, over-award payments, and so on, rather than equal pay is stressed here. Performance or merit-based

pay, payment systems based on years of service (where this is shown to be relevant to job performance), and other individual-based payment systems, if not directly or indirectly related to sex of the employee, could result in variations in pay for jobs within the same grade or classification without this constituting sex discrimination.

10 Very few recommendations for job evaluation practice are included in this chapter. Detailed guidelines for acceptable practice in the Australian affirmative action environment are provided in the recommendations chapter of Burton et al., 1987. Fonda et al. 1979 provides a useful series of checklists.

11 For example, the Hay-MSL Code of Practice (available from the Hay-MSL Management Consultant Group, London).

Equal opportunities and equal pay for work of equal value in Australia

1 See *Ansett Transport Industries (Operations) Pty Ltd v. Wardley* (1980) 142 CLR 237; *Allders International Pty Ltd v. Anstee* (1986) 5 NSWLR 47; *Public Service Board of NSW v. Napier & Ors* (1984) EOC 92–134; *Squires v. Qantas Airways Ltd* (1985) EOC 92–135; *Thompson & Ors v. Qantas Airways Ltd.* (1989) EOC 92–251.

2 *Conciliation and Arbitration Act* 1904; *Industrial Arbitration Act* 1940 (NSW); *Industrial Relations Act* 1981 (Vic.); *Industrial Conciliation and Arbitration Act* 1961 (Qld); *Industrial Relations Act* 1985 (WA); *Industrial Relations Act* 1984 (Tas.); *Industrial Conciliation and Arbitration Act* 1972 (SA).

3 See, however, *ICA Act* 1961 (Qld) section 12 (1) (a) (i) which requires the Queensland Industrial Commission to fix wages on the basis of equal pay for work of equal value.

4 *NSW State Equal Pay Case* 1973 73 AR 425; *Clerks (Equal Pay) Case* 42 SAIR 943.

5 See Directive on Equal Pay (Council Directive No 75/117 EEC); *The Commission v. the United Kingdom Case 61/81* (1982) 3 CMLR 284

6 Canadian *Human Rights Act* 1977; *Pay Equity Act* 1988 Ontario; *Pay Equity Act* 1985 Manitoba.

7 *Sex Discrimination Act* 1984 (Cwlth); *Anti-Discrimination Act* 1977 (NSW); Equal Opportunity Acts 1984 (WA, SA and Vic.)

8 See for example, *Public Service Board of NSW v. Napier* (1984) EOC 92–134; *Koh v. Mitsubishi Motors Ltd* (1985) EOC 92–134; ct *Thompson & Ors v. Qantas Airways* (1989) EOC 92–251.

9 *Sex Discrimination Act* 1984 (Cwlth), s.40(1); *Equal Opportunity Act* 1984 (Vic.), ss.39(e), 21(4) (d); *Anti-Discrimination Act* 1977 (NSW), s.54(1).

10 *Equal Opportunity Act* 1984 (SA), *Equal Opportunity Act* 1984 (WA).

11 For a recent example of anti-discrimination legislation operating to effect the variation of an award see *Confederation of WA Industry Inc. v. The Trades and Labor Council*, CCH Australia and New Zealand Equal Opportunity Law and Practice, Report No.22, 1 March 1988.

12 *Termination Change and Redundancy Case* 9 IR 115.

13 *Human Rights and Equal Opportunity Commission Act* 1986 (Cwlth), s.11(1).

Bibliography

ACTU (1983a) *Working Women's Policy* Melbourne: ACTU
—— (1983b) *Working Women's Charter* Melbourne: ACTU
—— (1984) *Action Program for Women Workers* Melbourne: ACTU
—— (1985) *Working Women's Charter: Implementation Manual No. 2: Equal Pay* Melbourne: ACTU
—— (1987) *Equal Pay for Work of Equal Value: criteria for establishing a pay claim* Melbourne: ACTU
Affirmative Action Agency (1988) 'Affirmative action in the Metals Award restructure' Sydney: Affirmative Action Agency
Anselme, M. and R. Weisz (1985) 'Good Jobs and Bad: a differentiated structuring of the labour market' *Acta Sociologica* 28, 1, pp. 35–53
Ashridge Management College (1980) *Employee Potential: issues in the development of women* London: Institute of Personnel Management
Attwood, Margaret and Frances Hatton (1983) '"Getting On": Gender Differences in Career Development' in Gamarnikow et al. *Gender, Class and Work*
Bailey, John (1983) *Job Design and Work Organization: matching people and technology for productivity and employee involvement* Englewood Cliffs, NJ: Prentice-Hall
Baron, James N., Alison Davis-Blake and William T. Bielby (1986) 'The structure of opportunity: how promotion ladders vary within and among organizations' *Administrative Science Quarterly* 31, June, pp. 248–73
Bellak, Alvin, Marsh Bates and Daniel Glasner (1983) 'Job evaluation: its role in the comparable worth debate' *Public Personnel Management* 12, 4, pp. 418–24
Bennett, Laura (1984) 'The Construction of Skill: craft unions, women workers and the Conciliation and Arbitration Court' *Law in Context* 2, pp. 118–32
Benokraitis, Nijole V. and Joe R. Feagin (1978) *Affirmative Action and Equal Opportunity: Action, Inaction and Reaction* Boulder, Colorado: Westview Press
Bergmann, Barbara R. and William Darity (1980) 'Social Relations in the Workplace and Employer Discrimination', Industrial Relations Research Association, Proceedings of the 33rd Annual Meeting, pp. 155–62

Berlew, D. E. and D. T. Hall (1966) 'The Socialization of Managers: Effects of Expectations on Performance' *Administrative Science Quarterly* 11, 2, pp. 207–224

Block, David (1987) *Report by Efficiency Scrutiny Unit on Proposed Successor Arrangements to the Public Service Board* Canberra: Efficiency Scrutiny Unit

Bond, J.R. and W.E. Vinacke (1961) 'Coalitions in Mixed-Sex Triads' *Sociometry* 24

Bond, Roger (1987) 'Academic performance appraisal: velvet glove or iron fist?' *Journal of Tertiary Educational Administration* 9, 1, pp. 43–49

Bourdieu, Pierre (1977) *Outline of a Theory of Practice* Cambridge University Press

Bowman, Garda W. et al. (1965) 'Are Women Executives People?' *Harvard Business Review* 43, July–August

Brinkerhoff, Derick W. and Rosabeth Moss Kanter (1980) 'Appraising the performance of performance appraisal' *Sloan Management Review* Spring, pp. 3–14

Broadnax, Walter (1987) Paper presented at the OMCE comference, 'Ethics and Equity, October 9–11, Albany, New York

Brown, Clair and Joseph Pechman (eds) (1987) *Gender in the Workplace* Washington, DC: Brookings Institution

Brown, Richard Harvey (1978) 'Bureaucracy as Praxis: toward a political phenomenology of formal organizations' *Administrative Science Quarterly* 23, September, pp. 365–82

——(1984) 'Women as Employees: social consciousness and collective action' in Janet Siltanen and Michelle Stanworth (eds) *Women and the Public Sphere: a critique of sociology and politics* New York: St Martin's Press

Burchett, Shelley R. and Kenneth P. De Meuse (1985) 'Performance appraisal and the law' *Personnel* 62, 7, pp. 29–37

Burton, Clare (1985) *Subordination: Feminism and Social Theory* Sydney: Allen & Unwin

Burton, Clare (1988) *Redefining Merit* Occasional Paper No. 2, Affirmative Action Agency Canberra: AGPS

Burton, Clare with Raven Hag and Gay Thompson (1987) *Women's Worth: pay equity and job evaluation in Australia* Canberra: AGPS

Buono, Anthony F. and Judith B. Kamm (1983) 'Marginality and the Organizational Socialization of Female Managers' *Human Relations* 36, 12, pp. 1125–40

Cadieux, Rita (1984) 'Canada's Equal Pay for Work of Equal Value Law' in Remick *Comparable Worth and Wage Discrimination*

Caplow, Theodore (1954) *The Sociology of Work* Connecticut: Greenwood Press

Cavendish, Ruth (1982) *Women on the Line* London: Routledge & Kegan Paul

Child, John (1984) *Organisation: a guide to problems and practice* 2nd edn, London: Harper & Row

Cleverley, Graham (1971) *Managers and Magic* London: Longman

Cockburn, Cynthia (1981) 'The Material of Male Power' *Feminist Review* 9, October, pp. 41–58

——(1983) *Brothers: male dominance and technological change* London: Pluto Press

——(1985) *Machinery of Dominance: women, men and technical know-how* London: Pluto Press

——(1986) 'Women and Technology: opportunity is not enough' in Purcell et al. *The Changing Experience of Employment*

Cohen, Yinon and Jeffrey Pfeffer (1986) 'Organizational Hiring Standards' *Administrative Science Quarterly* 32, pp. 1–24

Collinson, David and David Knights (1986) '"Men Only": theories and practices of job segregation in insurance' in Knights and Willmott *Gender and the Labour Process*

Commission for Racial Equality (1983) *Code of Practice for the elimination of racial discrimination and the promotion of equality of opportunity in employment* London: HMSO

Connell, R.W. (1983) *Which Way is Up? Essays on Class, Sex and Culture* Sydney: Allen & Unwin

—— (1987) *Gender and Power* Sydney: Allen & Unwin

Cook, Alice H. (1985) *Comparable Worth: a case book of experiences in states and localities* University of Hawaii at Manoa: Industrial Relations Centre (Supplement 1986)

Coombs Report (1976) *Royal Commission on Australian Government Administration Report* Canberra: AGPS

Cox, Taylor, Jr and Stella M. Nkomo (1986) 'Differential performance appraisal criteria: a field study of black and white managers' *Group and Organization Studies* 11, 1–2, pp. 101-119

Crompton, Rosemary and Gareth Jones (1984) *White-Collar Proletariat: deskilling and gender in clerical work* London: Macmillan

Curtain, Richard (1987) 'Skill formation and the enterprise' *Labour and Industry* 1, 1, pp. 8–38

Davies, Celia and Jane Rosser (1986) 'Gendered Jobs in the Health Service: a problem for labour process analysis' in Knights and Willmott *Gender and the Labour Process*

Deacon, Desley (1983) 'Women, bureaucracy and the dual labour market: an historical analysis' in Alexander Kouzmin (ed.) *Public Sector Administration: New Perspectives* Melbourne: Longman Cheshire

DEIR (Department of Employment and Industrial Relations (Cwlth) (1985) *Report to the International Labour Organisation* (re the ILO Equal Remuneration Convention, 1951, No. 100), Canberra

Dipboye, Robert L. (1985) 'Some neglected variables in research on discrimination in appraisals' *Academy of Management Review* 10, 1, pp. 116–27

Duster, Troy (1976) 'The Structure of Privilege and its Universe of Discourse' *American Sociologist* 11 (May) 73–78

Edelman, Murray (1974) *The Symbolic Uses of Politics* University of Illinois Press

Edwards, Mark R. and Ruth J. Sproull (1985) 'Safeguarding your employee rating system' *Business* April–June, pp. 17–27

Eisenstein, Hester (1985) 'The Gender of Bureaucracy: reflections on feminism and the state' in Jacqueline Goodnow and Carole Pateman (eds) *Women, Social Science and Public Policy* Sydney: Allen & Unwin

Elizur, Dov (1987) *Systematic Job Evaluation and Comparable Worth* Aldershot, Hampshire: Gower

Elshtain, Jean Bethke (1981) *Public Man, Private Woman: Women in Social and Political Thought* New Jersey: Princeton University Press

Equal Employment Opportunity Commission (1978) 'Adoption of four agencies of uniform guidelines on employee selection procedures' *Federal Register* 25 August, vol. 43, 38290–38315

Equal Opportunities Commission (1985a) *Code of Practice for the elimination of discrimination on the grounds of sex and marriage and the promotion of equality of opportunity in employment* London: HMSO

—— (1985b) *Job Evaluation Schemes Free of Sex Bias* Manchester: Equal Opportunities Commission

Equal Opportunities Review (1988a) 'New job evaluation benefits women at Save the Children Fund' 17, January–February

Evans, Sara M. and Barbara J. Nelson (1988) 'Comparable Worth: the paradox of technocratic reform' *Feminist Studies* 14

—— (1988b) 'Advertising Equality' 22, November–December, pp. 15–18

Fear, Richard and James Ross (1983) *Jobs, Dollars and EEO: how to hire more productive entry-level workers* New York: McGraw-Hill

Feild, Hubert S. and William H. Holley (1982) 'The relationship of performance appraisal system characteristics to verdicts in selected employment discrimination cases' *Academy of Management Journal* 25, 2, pp. 392–406

Ferguson, Kathy (1984) *The Feminist Case against Bureaucracy* Philadelphia: Temple University Press

Ferraro, Geraldine A. (1984) 'Bridging the Wage Gap: Pay Equity and Job Evaluations' *American Psychologist* 39, 10, pp. 1166–70

Fonda, Nickie, Pauline Glucklich, Janet Goodman and Janice Morgan (1979) 'Job evaluation without sex discrimination' *Personnel Management* 11, 2, pp. 34–7, 43

Fouracre, Sandra (1984) 'Equal value and job evaluation' *Topics* July, Cambridge: Employment Resource Centre, reprinted by Hay-MSL, London

Gamarnikow, Eva, David Morgan, June Purvis and Daphne Taylorson (eds) (1983) *Gender, Class and Work* London: Heinemann

Game, Ann (1984) 'Affirmative Action: liberal rationality or challenge to patriarchy?' *Legal Services Bulletin* 9, 6, pp. 253–57

Game, Ann and Rosemary Pringle (1983) *Gender at Work* Sydney: Allen & Unwin

Geis, A. Arthur (1987) 'Making merit pay work' *Personnel* January, pp. 52–60

Gillett, Ross (1987) Job evaluation: a general introduction, unpublished paper, Women's Policy Coordination Unit, Department of the Premier and Cabinet, Victoria

Goddard, Robert W. (1985) 'The '80s employee' *Management World* 14, 4, pp. 8–10

Goffman, Erving (1979) *Gender Advertisements* London: Macmillan

Grams, R. and D. Schwab (1985) 'Systematic sex-related error in job evaluation' *Academy of Management Journal* 28, 2, pp. 279–90

Greenhalgh, Roger (1987) 'Equal Opportunities' in Sally Harper (ed.) *Personnel Management Handbook* Aldershot, Hampshire: Gower

Greenwood, Daphne (1984) 'The Institutional Inadequacy of the Market in Determining Comparable Worth: Implications for Value Theory' *Journal of Economic Issues* 18, 2, pp. 457–64

Gregory, R.G. and R.G. Duncan (1981) 'Segmented Labour Market Theories and the Australian Experience of Equal Pay for Women' *Journal of Post-Keynesian Economics* 3, Spring, pp. 403–28

Gregory, R.G. and V. Ho (1985) 'Equal Pay and Comparable Worth: what can the U.S. learn from the Australian experience?' Discussion Paper No. 123, July, Australian National University: Centre for Economic Policy Research

Grey, Nicholas (1988) 'Pay Equity for Social Workers' *Federal Industrial News* (Journal of the Professional Officers' Association) 42, March, pp. 1ff.

Hackman, J.R. and G. Oldham (1980) *Work Redesign* Reading, Mass.: Addison-Wesley

Halachmi, Arie and Marc Holzer (1987) 'Merit pay, performance targeting and productivity' *Review of Public Personnel Administration* 7, 2, pp. 80–91

Harmon, M. (1974) 'Social equity and organizational man: motivation and organizational democracy' *Public Administrative Review* January–February, pp. 11–18

—— (1981) *Action Theory for Public Administration* London: Longman

Hartmann, Heidi (ed.) (1985) *Comparable Worth: new directions for research* Washington, DC: National Academy Press

—— (1987) 'Internal Labor Markets and Gender: a case study of promotion' in Brown and Pechman *Gender in the Workplace*

Hawkesworth, Mary E. (1984) 'The Affirmative Action Debate and Conflicting Conceptions of Individuality' *Women's Studies International Forum* 7, 5, pp. 335–47

Hearn, Jeff and Wendy Parkin (1987) *'Sex' at 'Work': the power and paradox of organisation sexuality* Brighton, Sussex: Wheatsheaf Books

Heritage, John (1983) 'Feminisation and Unionisation: a case study from banking' in Gamarnikow et al. *Gender, Class and Work*

Heydebrand, Wolf V. (1983) 'Technocratic Corporatism: toward a theory of occupational and organizational transformation' in Richard Hall and Robert Quinn (eds) *Organizational Theory and Public Policy* London: Sage Publications

Hill, Michael (1972) *The Sociology of Public Administration* London: Weidenfeld & Nicolson

Holden, Matthew (1973) *The White Man's Burden* New York: Chandler

Hughes, Everett (1944) 'Dilemmas and Contradictions of Status *American Journal of Sociology* 50, pp. 353–9

Hunt, Audrey (1975) *Management Attitudes and Practices Towards Women at Work* London: HMSO

Hunter, Rosemary (1988) Legal Intervention in Australian Employment Relations: the case of indirect discrimination, unpublished research project, Faculty of Law, University of Melbourne

Hyman, Prue (1987) Equal pay for work of equal value—job evaluation issues, paper presented to the Third Conference on Labour, Employment and Work, Victoria University of Wellington, October

International Labour Organisation (1960) *Job Evaluation* Geneva: International Labour Office

Izraeli, Dafna N. and Dove Izraeli (1985) 'Sex effects in evaluating leaders: a replication study' *Journal of Applied Psychology* 70, 3, pp. 540—46

Janner, Greville (1988) 'Individual rights at work' in Bryan Livy (ed.) *Corporate Personnel Management* London: Pitman

Janson, R. (1975) 'A job enrichment trial in data processing—in an insurance organization' in L.E. Davis and A.B. Cherns (eds) *The Quality of Working Life* vol. 2, New York: Free Press

Jenkins, Richard (1987) 'Equal Opportunity in the Private Sector: the limits of voluntarism' in Richard Jenkins and John Solomos (eds) *Racism and Equal Opportunity Policies in the 1980s* Cambridge University Press

Kane, Jeffrey S. and Edward E. Lawler (1979) 'Performance appraisal effectiveness: its assessment and determinants' *Research in Organizational Behavior* 1, pp. 425—78

Kanter, Rosabeth (1977) *Men and Women of the Corporation* New York: Basic Books

—— (1980) 'The Impact of Organization Structure: Models and Methods for Change' in Ronnie Steinberg Ratner (ed.) *Equal Employment Policy for Women* Philadelphia: Temple University Press

—— (1983) *The Change Masters: corporate entrepreneurs at work* London: Unwin Paperbacks

Kelley, Maryellen R. (1984) 'Commentary: the need to study the transformation of job structures' in Reskin *Sex Segmentation in the Workplace*

—— (1987) Comments on 'Internal Labor Markets and Gender' in Brown and Pechman *Gender in the Workplace*

Kessler, S., D.J. Ashenden, R.W. Connell and G.W. Dowsett (1985) 'Gender Relations in Secondary Schooling' *Sociology of Education* 58, January, pp. 34—48

King, Kathleen and Ann F. Hoffman (1984) 'Comparable Worth: a trade union issue' *Women's Rights Law Reporter* 8, pp. 95—107

Kingston, Beverley (1981) 'Women and Equity in Australia' in P.N. Troy (ed.) *A Just Society?* Sydney: Allen & Unwin

Klasson, Charles R., Duane E. Thompson and Gary L. Luben (1980) 'How defensible is your performance appraisal system?' *Personnel Administration* 25, 12, pp. 77—83

Kleiman, L.S. and R.L. Durham (1981) 'Performance appraisal, promotion and the courts: a critical review' *Personnel Psychology* 34, pp. 103—21

Knights, David and Hugh Willmott (1986) *Gender and the Labour Process* Introduction, Aldershot, Hampshire: Gower

Kraiger, Kurt and J. Kevin Ford (1985) 'A meta-analysis of ratee race effects in performance rating' *Journal of Applied Psychology* 70, 1, pp. 56—65

Kranz, Harry (1974) Are merit and equity compatible?' *Public Administration Review* vol 34 No 5 pp. 434—440

—— (1976) *The Participatory Bureaucracy* Lexington, Mass.: Lexington Books

Lansbury, Russell D. (ed.) (1981) *Performance Appraisal* Melbourne: Macmillan

Lansbury, R.D. and P. Gilmour (1986) 'Supervisors and Industrial Democracy: forces for reaction or reform?' in Ed Davis and Russell Lansbury (eds) *Democracy and Control in the Workplace* Melbourne: Longman Cheshire

Lazer, Robert I. (1976) 'The "discrimination" danger in performance appraisal' *Conference Board Record* March, pp. 60–64

Lenney, Ellen, Linda Mitchell and Chris Browning (1983) 'The effect of clear evaluation criteria on sex bias in judgments of performance' *Psychology of Women Quarterly* 7, 4, pp. 313–28

Lipman-Blumen, Jean (1976) 'Toward a Homosocial Theory of Sex Roles: An Explanation of the Sex Segregation of Social Institutions' in Martha Blaxall and Barbara Reagan (eds) *Women and the Workplace* University of Chicago Press

Livernash, E. Robert (1980) 'An overview' in E. Robert Livernash (ed.) *Comparable Worth: issues and alternatives* Washington, DC: Equal Employment Advisory Council

Livy, Bryan (1975) *Job Evaluation: a critical review* London: George Allen & Unwin

—— (1988a) 'Performance appraisal, assessment centres and management development' in Bryan Livy (ed.) *Corporate Personnel Management* London: Pitman

Livy, Bryan (1988b) 'Job evaluation' in Bryan Livy (ed.) *Corporate Personnel Management* London: Pitman

Loring, R. and T. Wells (1972) *Breakthrough: Women into Management* New York: Von Nostrand Reinhold Co.

Lubben, Gary L., Duane E. Thompson and Charles R. Klasson (1980) 'Performance appraisal: the legal implications of Title VII' *Personnel* 57, 3, pp. 11–21

Lyle, Jerolyn and Jane Ross (1973) *Women in Industry* Lexington, Mass.: Lexington Books

Maguire, Michael (1986) 'Recruitment as a Means of Control' in Purcell et al. *The Changing Experience of Employment*

Major, Klaus (1984) Staff training and development practitioners: a labour market analysis, paper presented in the unit 'Individual and Organisation', Kuring-gai College of Advanced Education

—— (1985) Study Assistance in a Commonwealth Department: Different Gender, Different Benefits, paper presented in the unit 'Managing Discrimination', Kuring-gai College of Advanced Education

Manwaring, Tony and Stephen Wood (1985) 'The Ghost in the Labour Process' in David Knights, Hugh Willmott and David Collinson (eds) *Job Redesign: critical perspectives on the labour process* Aldershot, Hampshire: Gower

Marshall, Judi (1984) *Women Managers: travellers in a male world* New York: John Wiley

Martin, David C., Kathryn M. Bartol and Marvin J. Levine (1986–87) 'The legal ramifications of performance appraisal' *Employee Relations Law Journal* 12, 3, pp. 370–96

McArthur, Leslie (1985) 'Social judgment biases in comparable worth analysis' in Hartmann *Comparable Worth*

McCarthy, Terence E. and Raymond J. Stone (1986) *Personnel Management in Australia* Brisbane: John Wiley

McEnery, Jean and Mark Lifter (1987) 'Demands for change: interfacing environmental pressures and the personnel process' *Public Personnel Management* 16, 1, pp. 61–87

McGavin, P.A. (1983) 'Equal Pay for Women: a re-assessment of the Australian experience' *Australian Economic Papers* 22, June, pp. 48–59

McLane, Helen J. (1980) *Selecting, Developing and Retaining Women Executives: a corporate strategy for the eighties* New York: Van Nostrand Reinhold Co.

Meade, Marvin (1971) '"Participative" administration—emerging reality or wishful thinking?' in Dwight Waldo (ed.) *Public Administration in a Time of Turbulence* Novato, Calif.: Chandler and Sharp Publishers

Miller, Jon (1986) *Pathways in the Workplace: the effects of gender and race on access to organizational resources* Cambridge University Press

Moore, Wilbert (1962) *The Conduct of the Corporation* New York: Random House

Morgan, Gareth (1986) *Images of Organization* London: Sage Publications

Mosher, Frederick (1968) *Democracy and the Public Service* Oxford University Press

MR (1982) Causes and Effects of Occupational Streaming within the Administrative and Clerical Division of the NSW Public Service, paper presented in the unit 'Individual and Organisation', Kuring-gai College of Advanced Education

National Pay Equity Coalition (1988) *Submission to the 1988 National Wage Case* Melbourne, 16 June

Newman, Winn (1982) 'Pay Equity Emerges as a Top Labor Issue in the 1980s' *Monthly Labor Review* 105, 4, pp. 49–51

Nieva, Veronica F. and Barbara A. Gutek (1980) 'Sex Effects on Evaluation' *Academy of Management Review* 5, 2, pp. 167–76

Nisbet, Lee (1977) 'Affirmative Action—a Liberal Program?' in Barry R. Gross (ed.) *Reverse Discrimination* Buffalo, New York: Prometheus

O'Donnell, Carol (1984) *The Basis of the Bargain: gender, schooling and jobs* Sydney: Allen & Unwin

O'Donnell, Carol and Philippa Hall (1988) *Getting Equal: labour market regulation and women's work* Sydney: Allen & Unwin

O'Farrell, Brigid and Sharon L. Harlan (1984) 'Job integration strategies: today's programs and tomorrow's needs' in Reskin *Sex Segmentation in the Workplace*

Office of the Public Service Board (1987) *Participative Work Design* Canberra: AGPS

O'Leary, V. and R. Hansen (1982) 'Trying Hurts Women, Helps Men: the Meaning of Effort' in H.J. Bernardin (ed.) *Women in the Workforce* New York: Praeger

Ontario Women's Directorate (1988) *Questions and Answers: pay equity in the workplace* Toronto: Ontario Women's Directorate

Osterman, Paul (1984) 'White-collar Internal Labour Markets' in Paul Osterman (ed.) *Internal Labour Markets* Cambridge, Mass.: MIT Press

—— (1987) Comments on 'Internal Labour Markets and Gender' in Brown and Pechman *Gender in the Workplace*

Ouchi, William G. and Alan L. Wilkins (1985) 'Organizational Culture' *Annual Review of Sociology* 11, pp. 457–83

Pateman, Carole (1981) 'The Concept of Equity' in P.N. Troy (ed.) *A Just Society? Essays on Equity in Australia* Sydney: Allen & Unwin

—— (1983) The Impact of Feminism on Political Theory, paper presented to the 53rd ANZAAS Congress, Perth, May

Peters, T.J. and R.H. Waterman (1982) *In Search of Excellence* New York: Harper & Row

Pfeffer, Jeffrey and Alison Blake-Davis (1987) 'The Effect of the Proportion of Women on Salaries: the case of College administrators' *Administrative Science Quarterly* 32, pp. 1–24

Phillips, Anne and Barbara Taylor (1980) 'Sex and Skill: Notes Towards a Feminist Economics' *Feminist Review* 6, pp. 79–88

Phillips, Esther (1986) 'The role of guidance in managing change' *British Psychological Society Bulletin* 2, 4, pp. 4–7

PJ (1987) Essay presented in the unit 'Managing Discrimination', Kuring-gai College of Advanced Education

Podrebarac, George (1987) 'A Message from the Commissioner' *Pay Equity Newsletter* (Ontario) 1, 1

Pollert, Anna (1981) *Girls, Wives, Factory Lives* London: Macmillan

Powell, Susan (1988) 'Wage Gap Widening' *Australian Society* April

Public Service Board (1984) *Job Structures for Keyboard Work: new directions?* Canberra: Public Service Board

Purcell, Kate, Stephen Wood, Alan Waton and Sheila Allen (eds) (1986) *The Changing Experience of Employment: restructuring and recession* London: Macmillan

Reed, Rosslyn (1986) Making newspapers pay: employment of women's skills in newspaper production, paper presented to the Annual Meeting of the Australian and Pacific Researchers in Organisation Studies, University of Melbourne, May 16–18

Remick, Helen (ed.) (1984a) *Comparable Worth and Wage Discrimination: technical possibilities and political realities* Philadelphia: Temple University Press

Remick, Helen (1984b) 'Dilemmas of implementation: the case of nursing' in Remick *Comparable Worth and Wage Discrimination*

Remick, Helen (1984c) 'Major issues in *a priori* applications' in Remick *Comparable Worth and Wage Discrimination*

Reskin, Barbara (ed.) (1984) *Sex Segmentation in the Workplace: trends, explanations, remedies* Washington, DC: National Academy Press

Richards, Bob (1984) 'Is your performance-appraisal process ready to go to court? *Training* 21, 8, pp. 81–83

Robson, Peter (1978) 'Worker participation in Australia' *Current Affairs Bulletin* 1 March

Ronalds, Chris (1987) *Affirmative Action and Sex Discrimination: a handbook on legal rights for women* Sydney: Pluto Press

Roos, Patricia and Barbara Reskin (1984) 'Institutional factors contributing to sex segregation' in Reskin *Sex Segregation in the Workplace*

Rose, M. and B. Jones (1985) 'Managerial strategy and trade union responses in work reorganisation schemes at establishment level' in Knights et al. *Job Redesign*

Rosenbaum, James E. (1979) 'Tournament Mobility: Career Patterns in a Corporation' *Administrative Science Quarterly* 24, June, pp. 220–41

—— (1980) 'Hierarchical and Individual Effects on Earnings' *Industrial Relations* 19, 1, pp. 1–14

—— (1984) *Career Mobility in a Corporate Hierarchy* Orlando, Fla.: Academic Press

—— (1985) 'Jobs, Job Status and Women's Gains from Affirmative Action: Implications for Comparable Worth' in Hartmann *Comparable Worth*

Rubenstein, Michael (1984) *Equal Pay for Work of Equal Value: the new regulations and their implications* London: Macmillan

Ruble, Thomas L., Renae Cohen and Diane N. Ruble (1984) 'Sex Stereotypes: Occupational Barriers for Women' *American Behavioral Scientist* 27, 3, pp. 339–56

Ryan, Edna (1988) 'Equal Pay, Comparable Worth and the Central Wage Fixing System' *Australian Feminist Studies* 6, Autumn, pp. 7–15

Ryan, Edna and Anne Conlon (1975) *Gentle Invaders: Australian Women at Work 1788–1974*. Melbourne: Nelson

Ryan, Paul (1981) 'Segmentation, Duality and the Internal Labour Market' in Frank Wilkinson (ed.) *The Dynamics of Labour Market Segmentation* New York: Academic Press

Schneier, Craig Eric, Richard W. Beatty and Lloyd S. Baird (1986) 'How to construct a successful performance appraisal system' *Training and Development Journal* April, pp. 30–42

Schneier, Dena B. (1978) 'The impact of EEO legislation on performance appraisals' *Personnel* 55, 4, pp. 24–34

Schrank, Harris T. and John W. Riley (1976) 'Women in Work Organisations' in Juanita M. Kreps (ed.) *Women and the American Economy: a Look to the 1980s* Englewood Cliffs, New Jersey: Prentice-Hall

Schuler, Randall S. and Stuart A. Youngblood (1986) *Effective Personnel Management* 2nd edn, New York: West Publishing

Seear, The Baroness (1988) 'Developing Positive Policies' in Livy *Corporate Personnel Management*

SEIU (Service Employees International Union) (1985) *Pay Equity Bargaining Guide* 2 vols. Contact: 1313 L Street, NW Washington, DC 20005

Shepela, Sharon Toffey and Ann T. Viviano (1984) 'Some Psychological Factors Affecting Job Segregation and Wages' in Remick *Comparable Worth*

Sheriff, P.E. (1974) 'Unrepresentative bureaucracy' *Sociology* 8, 3, pp. 447–62

Short, C. (1986) 'Equal Pay—What Happened?' *Journal of Industrial Relations* 28, 3, PP. 315–35

Sigelman, Lee, H. Brinton Milward and Jon M. Shepard (1982) 'The Salary Differential between Male and Female Administrators: Equal Pay for Equal Work? *Academy of Management Journal* 25, 3, pp. 664–71

Sims, Ronald R., John G. Veres and Susan M. Heninger (1987) 'Training appraisers: an orientation program for improving supervisory performance ratings' *Public Personnel Management* 16, 1, pp. 37–46

Stace, Doug A. (1987) 'The value-added organisation: trends in Human Resource Management' *Human Resource Management Australia* November, pp. 52–63

Stanton, M.A. (1978) 'The Merit Principle: its history and future', Research Paper 2, Australian Public Service Board, Canberra: AGPS

Steinberg, Ronnie and Lois Haignere (1985) *Equitable Compensation: methodological criteria for comparable worth*, Working Paper No. 16, State University of New York at Albany: Center for Women in Government

Strober, Myra and Carolyn Arnold (1987) 'The dynamics of occupational segregation among bank tellers' in Brown and Pechman *Gender in the Workplace*

Subramanium, V. (1967) 'Representative bureaucracy: a reassessment'. *American Political Science Review* 61 1010–19.

Taylor, Patricia (1985) 'Institutional job training and inequality'. *Social Science Quarterly* Vol. 66 (March) pp. 67–78.

Tepperman, Jean (1976) *Not Servants, Not Machines: office workers speak out!* Boston: Beacon Press

Thomason, George F. (1980) *Job Evaluation: objectives and methods* London: Institute of Personnel Management

Thompson, Michael (1982) 'A Three-Dimensional Model' in Mary Douglas (ed.) *Essays in the Sociology of Perception* London: Routledge & Kegan Paul

Treiman, Donald J. (1979) *Job Evaluation: an analytic review* Washington, DC: National Academy of Sciences

—— (1984) 'Effect of choice of factors and factor weights in job evaluation' in Remick *Comparable Worth and Wage Discrimination*

Treiman, Donald J. and Heidi I. Hartmann (1981) *Women, Work and Wages: equal pay for jobs of equal value* Washington, DC: National Academy Press

Van Maanen, John and Stephen R. Barley (1985) 'Cultural Organisation: fragments of a theory' in Peter Frost, Larry Moore, Meryl Louis, Craig Lundberg and Janne Martin (eds) *Organizational Culture* London: Sage Publications

Veiga, J. (1983) 'Mobility Influences during Managerial Career Stages' *Academy of Management Journal* 26, 1, pp. 64–85

Walden, Rosa and Ella Rosso (1985) 'Review of the Operation of the Merit Principle', Draft Report, Personnel Policy and Practices Branch, Public Service Board, Canberra

Walker, Patrick and Angela Bowey (1982) 'Sex discrimination and job evaluation' in Angela Bowey (ed.) *Handbook of Salary and Wage Systems* 2nd edn, Aldershot, Hampshire: Gower

White, Orion (1971) 'Social change and administrative adaptation.' in Frank Marini (ed.) *Toward a New Public Administration: the Minnowbrook Perspective.* Scranton: Chandler

Wilenski, Peter (1984) 'Equal Employment Opportunity — widening the agenda' Keynote address to the Equal Employment Opportunity Conference, 'Reshaping the Workplace', Sydney University, June 6

Wilenski, Peter (1986) *Public Power and Public Administration*, Sydney: Hale and Iremonger

Winters, Sylvia (1987) 'Career progression and restructuring' *ACOA Journal* No. 839 (Oct/Nov) pp. 12–13.

Women's Bureau (1988a) *OECD Report to the Working Party on the Role of Women in the Economy* Canberra: Department of Employment, Education and Training

—— (1988b) 'Jennie George Addresses Bureau Seminar' *Women and Work* 10, 1

Women's Electoral Lobby (1983) *Submission to the National Wage Case* Sydney: Women's Electoral Lobby

Zaleznick, Abraham and Manfred Kets de Vries (1975) *Power and the Corporate Mind* Boston: Houghton Mifflin Co.

Ziller, Alison (1980) *Affirmative Action Handbook* Sydney: NSW Government Printer

Index

132−3, 134−5, 137, 145, 146; *see also* National wage-fixing principles

National wage-fixing principles, 89, 128, 133, 134, 136, 137, 138, 144, 148

'natural' female attributes, 26, 99, 113; *see also* skills; women

negotiation, between organisation and job evaluation consultant, 107−13; and job evaluation, 97, 98; of meaning, 47, 48; in organisations, 9; and representativeness, 40

New Public Administration, 39, 40, 47

New York Civil Service Commission, 55

New York State, 55

New Zealand, 55

Newman, W., 16, 66

Nieva, V.F., 18, 83, 84

Nisbet, L., 15

Nkomo, S.M., 69, 83

Nord v. US Steel Corp., 84

nurses, and comparable worth, 132−6; education of, 136, 139−40; and maintenance fitters, 96; professional status of, 139, 140; and tree trimmers, 105

Nurses' Case, 135−6, 138, 140

occupational groups, 51; and pay cases, 135−40; *see also* occupations, power of; sex segregation

occupational hierarchies, 86; *see also* occupations; sex segregation

occupational segregation, 6, 77; patterns of, 79; *see also* sex segregation

occupational strategies, 50

occupational structures, 12; *see also* occupations

occupational therapists, *see* therapists

occupations, female-dominated, 94, 102, 105, 135, 144; male-dominated, 94, 105, 133, 136,

144; *see also* classifications; jobs; sex segregation

O'Donnell, C., xi, 26, 128, 146, 149

OECD Report to the Working Party on the Role of Women in the Economy, 129

O'Farrell, B., 60, 73

Office of Equality in Employment, 53

office restructuring, 73; *see also* job redesign; work reorganisation

older workers, xi

Oldham, G., 63, 69, 72

O'Leary, V., 18, 26

Ontario, 134, 142

Ontario, Women's Directorate, 99

opportunities, access to, 10; allocation of, 22; distribution of, 21, 22; structuring of, 14, 15, 22, 50, 73

opportunity structures, 65, 73; shape of, 22

Oregon public service, 108, 109

organisation design, 63

organisational change, and EEO, 34−6; *see also* organisations; work reorganisation

organisational cultures, 31−4, 65, 95, 106, 112, 113; and women's marginal place, 32; *see also* organisational values

organisational politics, 3, 102; *see also* organisations

organisational rewards, 7, 8, 10, 12, 15, 22

organisational structures, 12, 48

organisational values, 51, 56, 59, 80, 95, 112, 113; 'capturing of', 102, 103; *see also* organisational cultures; value consensus

organisations, 'domestic' work in, 26; 'fitting into', 5, 22, 33, 83; gender structuring of, 35, 62; and masculine values, 3−23; myth of, 30−1; as political entities, 30−1; power, 3−23, 30, 51, 73, 104; as rational, 30−1, 33, 34, 145; and as sites of socialisation, 34

Osterman, P., 35

affirmative action in, x, 55, 81; firms, 31, 74, 94; job evaluation in, 88, 105, 108; management, 35; masculine values in, xi; organisations, 34; recruiting from, 44

productivity, and discrimination, 21, 73; and EEO, 90; and individual effort, 18; and organisational change, 35; and representativeness, 40–1; and work reorganisation, 61

professional associations, 14, 50

Professional Engineers' Case, 140

Professional Officers' Association (POA), 136, 137, 138, 139

professional staff, 112

'professionalising', 51

programming work, 64

promotion, access to, 89; decisions, 72, 83; and EEO, 22, 24, 39, 52, 58; and geographic mobility; ladders, 62; of men and women, 35, 50, 119; opportunities, 115; changes in, 49; and performance assessment, 76, 80, 84; potential, 79; promotional patterns, 13; promotional position, 26; women and, 10

protective strategies, 51

psychologists, 137, 138

public administration, 40, 41; education, 50; literature, 39; reform, 39

public contact work, 28, 69–70, 71, 98, 100, 108

public sector, x, xi, 4 *passim*, 76–90

Public Service Board (Australian), 66, 137; abolition of, 53; Office of the, 61; working parties of, 22, 39

Public Service Board (N.S.W.), 110

Public Service Board of NSW v. Napier & Ors, 154

Public Service Reform Act 1984 (Cwlth), 24, 131, 153

public sphere, and men, 32, 33; *see also* public/private domains

public/private domains, 7, 8, 12; *see*

also domestic sphere; public sphere

qualifications, comparable, 139–40; educational, 49, 138–40, 141, 143; and EEO, 87; job-related, 50; and the merit principle, 23, 24, 45; and pay equity, 77; for positions, 25, 49, 50; and work-value, 140, 144; *see also* merit

qualities, 23, 42, 87

Questions and Answers: pay equity in the workplace, 142

race, racial minorities, and diversity, 52; and indirect discrimination, 79; and job evaluation, 110; and merit, 124; and organisational culture, 65, 69; and public contact positions, 69; and task allocation, 62; *see also* Aboriginal people; minority groups; people of non-English speaking background; race bias

race bias, in job design and job allocation, 63; in job evaluation, 80; in performance assessment, 77, 80, 82–6

racism, 40; racist views, 47

Rafferty, F., 137

reasonable adjustment, 64

receptionist, 36, 99, 106; duties, 70

recruitment, of Aboriginal people, 54; into clerical grades, 65, 118; decisions, 13; and discrimination, 16–17, 122–3; and diversity, 39, 49; and EEO, 52, 53, 58; and equity, 44; lateral, 51; in the 1990's, xi; *see also* job assignment

redundancy, 77, 84

Reed, R., 108

Remick, H., 97, 98, 99

repetitive work, 109; *see also* jobs, routine

Report of the Royal Commission on Public Service Administration, 4

representation, 41, 42, 47, 110;